Temp
By
Choice

By
Diane Thrailkill

CAREER PRESS
180 Fifth Avenue
P.O. Box 34
Hawthorne, NJ 07507
1-800-CAREER-1
201-427-0229 (outside U.S.)
FAX: 201-427-2037

9/96

#29521488

TEMP BY CHOICE

ISBN 1-56414-122-5, $10.95

Cover design by The Gottry Communications Group, Inc.

Printed in the U.S.A. by Book-mart Press

To order this title by mail, please include price as noted above, $2.50 handling per order, and $1.00 for each book ordered. Send to: Career Press, Inc., 180 Fifth Ave., P.O. Box 34, Hawthorne, NJ 07507

Or call toll-free 1-800-CAREER-1 (Canada: 201-427-0229) to order using VISA or MasterCard, or for further information on books from Career Press.

Library of Congress Cataloging-in-Publication Data

Thrailkill, Diane,
   Temp by choice / by Diane Thrailkill.
     p.   cm.
   Includes index.
   ISBN 1-56414-122-5 : $10.95
   1. Temporary employment. 2. Temporary employees. I. Title.
HD5854.T48   1994
331.25'72--dc20   93-45845
                                                     CIP

Dedication

To Susana, my friend and daughter.

Acknowledgments

Special thanks go to Henry Berry, my literary agent, for his belief in the project, his enthusiasm and unflagging efforts on my behalf.

Thanks to my editor Betsy Sheldon and her assistant Ellen Scher for their dedication and editing skill.

My thanks to Jennifer Atkinson for early feedback and a re-introduction to the comma; to Pauline Donner and Salena Burnette, for generously providing accurate industry information before I knew the "right" questions to ask.

Many people gave support and encouragement on the long road from concept to print. Please know that I am grateful for your contribution.

And, to all the temps who have shared their knowledge and stories with me go the biggest thanks of all.

Contents

....

Introduction
Temping: Everybody Wins   7

Chapter 1
**Welcome to Temping: Weighing the
      Possibilities**   15

Chapter 2
**Getting Started: Finding, Evaluating and
      Registering With Temporary Agencies**   27

Chapter 3
**Handling Your First Assignments
      Like a Pro**   44

Chapter 4
Managing Multiple Agency Relationships   60

Chapter 5
Maximizing On-The-Job Efficiency   71

Chapter 6
All Things Computer   82

Chapter 7
**The Home Office, and the Professional
    Who Works There**   95

Chapter 8
Temping for Supplemental Income   108

Chapter 9
Money Matters and the Temp   125

Chapter 10
Laws, Insurance, Taxes   144

Chapter 11
Benefits: Medical, Disability, Pensions   160

Conclusion
Good News/Bad News Revisited   172

Appendix
Resource List   173

About the Author   185

Index   187

Introduction

Temping:
Everybody Wins

··

"GM cuts 24,000 jobs"

"IBM cuts another 8,000 staff"

"Sears Roebuckling. Cuts 7,000 jobs, spends $60M on computer"

Foreboding headlines no longer strike the chord of terror in me they once did. I will never be "unemployed" again. For the past seven years I have worked as an office temp, using marketable skills that cut across industry lines. My financial well-being is not dependent on the fortunes of a particular company or industry.

Over the past few years, the employment market has changed drastically. Former job-based positions, such as vice president of communications, have become *skill-based* interim work for contract workers, consultants, project managers and temps. As a result, the mainstream media seem locked into portraying all contingent workers as society's downsized victims or, at the very least, workers who are settling for less. It completely misses the point that a large number of those who continue to temp may be *settling* for *different*. I became a temp by accident, but I have remained one by choice.

This book is about options and choice. Temping has opened my eyes to opportunities I would never have seen, much less considered. I've learned more about running a business working in the trenches with the troops, than I ever did as a member of management. It has served me well. I want it to serve others well, too.

I think of temping as an adventure, an opportunity for a varied and productive life *and* a way to earn money. Not everyone shares my vision.

Why do it at all?

"Why would anyone in their right mind want to be a temp?" asked a friend. I had told her that I was writing a book on the subject as well as giving seminars on how to do it successfully.

Seven years later, another friend still asks periodically if I have a "job" yet. When I respond, "I have many jobs, I'm a professional temp," he shakes his head in disbelief, convinced that "professional temp" is an oxymoron.

Obviously, some people haven't figured out that we are all temporary in this life, or that a rose by any other name might be called a consultant. Certainly, there are enough misperceptions about the occupation:

Temps are failures; misfits who can't hold a job.

Temps are flaky actors with their minds focused on their next audition.

Benefits to the temporary employee

Why, indeed, would anyone want to be a temp? As I see it, there are several good reasons. You can:

- Learn to expertly surf this "wave of the future" currently breaking on job shores. Companies continue to streamline their operations with layoffs and automation, utilizing temporary employees to staff up and down as their business needs dictate. They hire consultants on a project basis.

If companies are using contingent employees strategically, shouldn't you use employers the same way?

- Investigate an industry or a company thoroughly, as an insider, before making a career commitment.
- Earn money quickly, with a minimum investment of time and/or expense, as an emergency measure between jobs.
- Secure a permanent job. When temps work out well, companies often find or create a permanent position for them, not necessarily the one they were performing as a temp.
- Finance a fledgling consultancy while securing insider information about a company or an industry.
- Subsidize a new business startup, or the establishment of a career in the arts.
- Reenter the work force more readily after a long absence.
- Ease into retirement.
- Have diversity without commitment.

Now, let's look at some of the reasons for considering temporary work in a little more detail:

1. As an interim/emergency measure. Not all companies provide generous severance packages to their outplaced workers, or ample warning of impending layoffs. Employees who find themselves out of a job with little or no notice can register immediately with agencies, work the following day and have a paycheck within a week.

2. Investigating industries or companies before making a commitment. You want to go to law school and turn your liberal arts degree into gold? Your knowledge of lawyers comes from watching "L.A. Law"? Work with real-life lawyers for a while. See how they stack up to the "reel life" ones.

The cosmetics industry sounds glamorous and exciting, full of beautiful people? Spend a month working for one of the big houses and see what you think.

3. New business startup, career in the arts. It takes time to establish a new business—or a career as an artist, writer or actor. Overnight successes happen only in the movies. Especially in the early stages of these endeavors, you can earn an hourly rate as a temp to subsidize yourself. In addition to the money, you have the use of office facilities away from home. As the business or career takes off, there is the option to work fewer hours. You may be able to schedule your appointments, make telephone calls, build a client base while collecting an hourly rate, and have the flexibility to schedule client sales calls or auditions during working hours if you need to.

4. Reentering the work force after a long absence. Whether your family is grown, your marital status has changed or your spouse is out of work, here is a way to get a view of what many types of jobs are all about. You can ease back into the work force, and your maturity will work in your favor. There are even agencies that specialize in this market niche. A number of the large, national agencies have specialty divisions as well. Mature temps are highly regarded because of their experience, wisdom and work ethic.

5. Insider information. Freelance software trainer Dana Epifan periodically works as a temp. She does it as much for the information as she does for money. Dana feels temping is the best way to learn the practical applications for the many software packages she teaches. As a temp, she finds out first-hand what she *should* be teaching people to do their job better. She is a pro who has as much business as she cares to take.

6. Diversity without commitment. If work is how you earn money, not who you are; if you prefer projects that use a variety of skills, have a beginning, a middle and an end; if you don't like office politics or office parties, become a temp. Play the role of perennial bridesmaid, and ignore the responsibilities of a bride.

Benefits to companies

It goes without saying that companies benefit from using temporary employees. The obvious reasons are the monetary savings—no recruiting costs, no maintenance costs and no providing of benefits such as college tuition reimbursement, medical, dental and disability insurance. Companies can hire a temporary expert to do a particular job, another expert when different skills are needed. If one temp doesn't meet the expectations, he or she can be replaced with another.

There are other benefits not so readily apparent. Temporary workers bring with them the knowledge and experience gained from working for many companies and can offer valuable insights on how to do the job better. They are self-starters who can tackle a job with little explanation and no training. Often, they are efficiency experts if they are combining their temping with another activity. Their focus is more toward completing the project rather than bucking for a promotion or socializing.

The successful job search: True temp stories

Frank Joerss had been with one company for 20 years when he suddenly found himself out of a job. Frank found another job right away. However, within a year, that company downsized and, as last hired, he was first fired. So, Frank found another job. The same thing happened again. Then, Frank went to work for a telemarketing firm that went belly-up 16 months later. This time Frank didn't find another job right away.

At the time he attended one of my seminars, he had been unemployed four months, had no hot prospects for a job and was somewhat discouraged about what had happened to his "career" over the last few years. Frank has a financial background and knows a lot about computers. He's a fast, two-fingered typist, testing at 50 words per minute. He began working as a temp. He kept an open mind as he worked for a variety of companies—Reader's Digest, SONY, General Foods, Chesebrough-Pond and St. Joseph's Medical Center—in a variety of positions, including secretarial, financial, administrative and technical areas.

Several weeks after completing a one-week secretarial assignment at St. Joseph's, Frank was offered a full-time job as a wage and salary analyst. He accepted. That position led to another as hospital database manager. Frank says he would never have thought of working for a medical center. He credits temping with opening his mind to new opportunities as well as finding him a job.

Before her entire department was eliminated, Janice Joseph was an assistant vice president at Bankers Trust. On her second temp assignment, a three-month slot, she worked as the assistant to the president of K-III Magazine Corporation (*Seventeen, New York Magazine, Soap Opera Digest*, among others). The company offered the job to her on a full-time basis before the three months were up. She accepted. Temping opened up an opportunity in an industry she had not considered before. Temping got her an introduction to a "decision-maker," the president.

Andrew Kasaija has a scholarly, youthful appearance and a precise manner of speech that, at first, made me mistake him for a graduate student. He is an entrepreneur with a solid business background who began investing in the stock market while he was still a teenager. He grew up in Europe and Africa, the son of career diplomats, graduating from college with a degree in math and computer science. His first job after college was as a computer programmer, but he found it boring. So he used the profits from his teenage investing to go into business for himself, trading overseas in used computer hardware, precious gems and currency.

A number of factors having to do with foreign currency problems and the Recession led him to close his business after three years and take a permanent job. The job was short-lived; the company went out of business. Andrew found another job, but that company restructured its salary structure and commissions in such a way that there was little financial incentive to remain. Andrew left to go with a small company. The company was bought by a larger one and the management team let go.

Andrew found that there were few jobs to be had at his level of expertise, and none for the salary he expected. He began consulting, and that brought him to my seminar. He saw temporary employment as a way to upgrade and keep current his somewhat dated technical knowledge. He viewed temping as a means to earn money during the down time between consulting projects. Andrew says temping gave him the flexibility he needed to build his new business. Within a few months he landed a lucrative project that has led to other opportunities. He hasn't had much down time.

Andrew wants his college-age brother and sister to learn how to temp when they graduate so they will never face unemployment in an unstable economy. He expresses the hope that they will never look solely at conventional ways to earn money or nurture a business.

The emergency: My story

I became a temp in an emergency and have remained one by choice. Nine years ago, I found myself in a situation where I was being pushed out of my position at a major corporation because I was over 40. I happened to love my job so I fought back, thinking once it was noted how serious I was about my career, the corporate minions would back off. I was wrong. I was fired. I filed an age discrimination suit and fought for three years. I didn't find justice, but I did find *truth.*

Over the three years I was engaged in legal battle, I had started a consulting business, subsidized myself by holding down (sequentially, not simultaneously) three undemanding jobs. The last one was as the office manager for a newly formed investment banking partnership.

My employment with them lasted 90 days. They ended their partnership of six months one weekend and fired us on Monday with no notice, no severance pay and no payment of the "guaranteed bonus" that was one of the terms of my particular employment agreement. Along with the normal financial obligations of single parenthood, I had college tuition for my daughter. In desperation I became an office temporary because I needed income quickly. Not an auspicious beginning for a career change to what was to become one of the fastest-growing industry segments in America.

Why have I remained a temp? I began writing books. As I became more involved in the writing and my consulting business grew, I found I couldn't put in 60 hours a week for a client and still have energy enough to write. I also became used to having a personal life, and I liked it. I have settled into a lifestyle that includes teaching the temp seminars, writing fiction along with nonfiction, occasional computer consulting and flexible temping. Working as a temp takes nothing from me emotionally, yet it subsidizes work I care about passionately.

I treat my temping as a business. I've learned to do it in a well-organized and professional manner that translates into good assignments at top rates. That's the part I hope this book passes along: how to get the most money, the best jobs, while expending the least amount of effort it takes to do so, leaving time to pursue your *real* goals, whatever they might be.

And to do it with the peace of mind that comes from calling the shots in your life. Temping is skill-based, rather than job-based. That means your market value is tied to what you can do and what your skill set is, not to the business success of a particular company.

Nothing is perfect, however. There are minuses right along with the pluses of temping, such as the lack of job security and the misperceptions that some people have about temps. I go into these problems and others in Chapter 1, but, for now, let me tell you how to use the book to your best advantage.

How to use the book

Read the first four chapters for a general overview of temporary employment. Chapter 5 gives specific information on how to organize assignments to secure blocks of free time. In particular, managers will pick up valuable pointers on how to increase administrative productivity. The remaining chapters cover setting up and using a home office productively, using temporary employment to subsidize a new business startup or a job search, the financial and legal aspects of running temporary work as a small business, either alone or in conjunction with other business interests. A quick reading of them will give you a broad overview; their segmentation will make it easy to consult specific topics.

This book grew out of seminars I have been giving for the past four years. As the Recession deepened, more and more unemployed middle managers began attending the seminars to investigate this temping option. Professional temps attended to learn and to share tips on how to do it better.

Resources are listed by section and summarized in the appendix. The book incorporates a number of check lists to facilitate decision-making and organization. All check lists are as complete as I could make them, but they are designed as much as anything to get you thinking about how to expand them, then adapt personalized versions to your own situations.

Whether we like it or not, temporary employment is a fact of life in the 1990s—and beyond. It may not be your present career of choice, but in the next decade or two it is likely to be your career periodically. Use the information in this book to learn how to work it to your advantage. Temping well is the best revenge.

Chapter 1

Welcome to Temping: Weighing the Possibilities

....

The more you know about a subject, the more likely you are to make informed choices. And exercise caution where it is needed. Before we go into the mechanics of how to register for temporary work, or what to do when you actually get an assignment, I think a brief discussion is in order about the positive and negative aspects of temping, the amount of money you can earn, and what your start-up costs will be. Let's begin the orientation with something even more important, the elements that, in my opinion, are critical for success.

Ask 100 professional temps why they've chosen their path and you will get 100 different answers. Take a look at what makes them successful at it, and two elements stand out. The primary factors that separate the successful professional temp from the rest of the crowd are their skill-based mentality and their flexibility.

Time is money; temps sell their knowledge and skill by the hour. The successful ones maintain a constant awareness of the correlation of their time to remuneration.

The bad news

1. Job security: The lack thereof. In the world of temping, there is no such thing as job security, either in the duration of the assignment or in the work itself.

By the time a work order is placed with the agency and you appear on the scene, a company's needs may have changed. The agency selected you because of your skill with computers and your knowledge of five software packages. You arrive at the company to find the job is photocopying a manual—at least for the first hour.

Perhaps you were selected because of your financial background and facility with spreadsheets. However, upon arrival you find the computer and desk you were to use have been usurped by another department. But that's okay, the numbers didn't arrive by overnight delivery either and, anyway, you're needed to deliver some mechanicals to the printer down the street. (The good news here is, although both jobs became unskilled labor for a period, you are still paid your premium rate.)

Your two-day assignment could end abruptly at 5:30 p.m. the first day because you finished all of the work they thought it would take two days to do. Or you can show up for an assignment and find out it was canceled earlier that morning while you were in transit and no one could reach you.

This is why the work is called "temporary." As a temp, your biggest appeal is that you are expendable. Always remember this and use it to your advantage. Don't misplace your loyalties.

By the way, finding out upon arrival that the assignment is canceled is an infrequent occurrence. It has happened to me three times in seven years. The agency will try to reassign you to another job immediately, of course. However, if work doesn't materialize, you're entitled to a half-day's pay from the agency. Do not work again for agencies who do not honor this standard.

2. Misperceptions of temps. Many unenlightened people think temps are unable to find or to hold a job. There are people who will not call you by name, but refer to you as "the temp," sometimes using the "third-person invisible," as in "Tell the temp I need this right away." You, the temp, are standing beside the person talking. I have been known to query in an impetuous moment, "Are you aware the temp can hear you?"

A frequent question asked at my seminars is, "Don't people treat you as a menial?" The answer is, "Occasionally." When I was an assistant vice president, there were people who treated me as a menial because I am female. It's the same mentality. The real question here is how do *you* define yourself? Are you a menial? Or, are you someone who may be doing work perceived by the functionally unenlightened as "menial" in order to earn money or gather information on your way toward another goal?

3. Lack of health benefits. Not many agencies provide medical and dental benefits, although more have begun to offer a somewhat limited medical insurance as temping becomes mainstream. The most common available medical coverage is through the National Association of Temporary Services (NATS). Its sponsored insurance is quite restricted, however.

From time to time, there has been talk of federal legislation requiring agencies to provide benefits. The current push to come up with a universal health care plan will certainly result in changes in the industry.

Some industry insiders predict that the high costs of various plans under consideration will have an end result of fewer full-time jobs. Companies will be disinclined to hire permanent employees because of the costs involved in furnishing medical insurance. One hopes the competition among forward-thinking temporary employment agencies will produce a vastly improved version over what is currently available.

Those people recently unemployed who were covered under a former employer's plan are entitled to 18 months of continuation insurance at group rates through the Consolidated Omnibus Reconciliation Act (COBRA).

Private insurance, when it is available, is not necessarily *always* prohibitive in cost. There are HMOs with individual plans available, organizations such as Co-Op America whose affiliation with Alternative Health Insurance Services (AHIS) provides affordable coverage to its members, and professional associations with member plans. For example, the National Writers Union is affiliated with the UAW. Its members have a group plan with Blue Cross/Blue Shield of Michigan.

In this book, Chapter 10 has detailed insurance information, including what to look for, how to evaluate policies under consideration and resources to help you find affordable insurance.

5. Onerous tasks. Every profession has its mundane tasks. Sometimes all the things the permanent employee hates to do are saved for the temp. The three leading favorites in the secretarial/administrative category are: 1) endless filing, 2) "doing a mailing" that involves collating copious amounts of material, stuffing it in envelopes and affixing the labels, and 3) photocopying items that have portions to be unstapled first, then put back in order and restapled.

6. Timesheets/paychecks. Keeping track of hours takes getting used to if you have always been paid based on an annual salary. Agencies use a timesheet to keep an accounting of your hours for their payroll. (See the example on the next page.) Copies serve as receipts to the client and to you. Timesheets are quadruplicate forms that must be filled out by you and signed by your supervisor. There is a place for the date or day of week, time started, time finished, meal breaks and total hours.

The agencies often have different days of the week designated as payday, and all have personalized timesheets. Some make the timesheet/payroll process easy for you. You call in your hours on Friday and drop off your timesheet when you pick up your check. Others do not make it easy, necessitating extra trips for you.

7. Miscellaneous annoyances. When you telephone the agencies to give your availability, you are almost always asked to list your skills as well. The person who takes this information may talk to more than 100 people a day—literally. He or she won't remember who you are, much less what you can do, so you recite. Working for several agencies means you go through this process with each one. I find it more of a tedious task than a time-consuming process.

Remember that your time is money—lunch with a friend "costs" an hour's pay.

Without a permanent home, there is no place to put personal belongings like toothbrush or reference books. I end up carrying everything with me.

LAUREN AND ASSOCIATES, INC.
Personnel Consultants

444 Park Avenue So., Suite 503, New York, NY 10016
Tel: 212 889-8869   Fax: 212 889-8912

EMPLOYER	
ADDRESS	
REPORT TO	TIME

I hereby certify that I have worked the hours shown hereon and they were worked by me during the week ending as designated and were certified by an authorized representative of the client firm. I understand that LAUREN AND ASSOCIATES, INC. reserves the right to pay me minimun wage if LAUREN AND ASSOCIATES, INC. is unable to bill their customer for total hours worked due to unsatisfactory job performance. I certify that no injuries other than those already reported to LAUREN AND ASSOCIATES, INC. were sustained during the assignment.

EMPLOYEE NAME (PLEASE PRINT)	EMPLOYEE NUMBER
SOCIAL SECURITY NUMBER	ORDER NUMBER
EMPLOYEE SIGNATURE	

DAY	MONTH/DATE	TIME IN	TIME OUT	LESS:LUNCH PERIOD	TOTAL HOURS
MON					
TUE					
WED					
THU					
FRI					
SAT					
SUN					
WEEK ENDING DATE (SUNDAY)	OFFICE I.D. NUMBER			TOTAL HOURS FOR WEEK	

FOUR HOUR MINIMUM PER EMPLOYEE PER DAY

CUSTOMER APPROVAL

Cross out any days not worked by employee. Approval includes verification of hours worked and acceptance of terms and conditions on reverse

X_____

RETURN TO LAUREN AND ASSOCIATES, INC.

Now, the good news

1. Minimal stress. At the end of the shift you walk out, and none of the work or worry goes with you. There is something clean about being paid for the amount of time you put in, walking away at the end of a day, and not taking problems with you.

You don't have to put up with abusive people. If you find yourself in a rotten situation, you can call the agency and get yourself replaced. You are no longer subject to the whims of some maniac in charge of your promotion or raise.

Removing yourself from the job should not be done frivolously. In seven years, I have done it three times. *Knowing* I can seems to be comfort enough for me in most instances.

2. Reduced expenses on wardrobe. You need fewer ensembles going from company to company. When you work for a company for no more than a week, no one need discover that you don't have a month's worth of smart-looking suits in your closet. Less money is spent on upkeep if you are able to wear washable clothes.

Corporate appearance, of course, is preferred, but it's a more relaxed corporate, and you can dress for the industry. In many Manhattan advertising agencies, for instance, the uniform runs more toward jeans combined with funky tops, or sweaters and sport coats rather than suits.

Depending on the assignment, women can skip the navy suit and stockings for pants; men can often forego ties. Never on the first day, though. It's always wise to dress professionally to make that first impression a strong one.

Whenever the agency sees you, you should dress corporate. No exceptions. You want to keep that image cemented in their collective minds. It will pay off in better jobs and higher hourly rates.

3. Diversity. Get an inside view of many industries and/or companies. Use your "invisible temp" status to observe working conditions and how they really treat people. Use multifarious skills in a variety of jobs while having an adventure. Imagine what you could learn about the inner workings of a magazine, even as an administrative assistant, if you worked in a different department each assignment. If you're more project-oriented than routine-oriented, you'll find that the variety of jobs, work environments and challenges offered by temping could be a permanent workstyle for you.

4. More personal flexibility. You have the ability to juggle your work schedule to accommodate your personal life. For instance, if you need to leave at 3 p.m. for an appointment, you can—without pay, of course. You may have blocks of time on the job where you can read, talk on the telephone, write letters, pay bills, learn software packages, study a subject or balance your checkbook. Your mind is free to think, plan and handle the details of your personal life or your new business.

Initially, it appalled me to learn that a position provided no work other than to occupy a desk for long periods, or to answer an occasional telephone call. In my opinion, far too many companies have pockets of incredible chaos in some of their divisions, or have supervisors who don't bother to plan the work for temps. When this happens with support staff, I call it the "secretary-as-ornament" syndrome. These situations, however inefficient they may be for the company, can be used to *your* personal advantage.

5. Overtime pay. Temps are paid for the actual hours worked, with time-and-a-half for anything over 40 hours. This is a federal law—the Fair Labor Standards Act: Minimum Wage and Overtime. It states that employees paid hourly are entitled to the applicable minimum wage and to time-and-a-half (premium pay) for every hour worked over 40 in one week, including work that would ordinarily be considered exempt on a full-time basis (accountant, technical trainer, etc.). Employees who are paid an hourly wage *must* be paid overtime.

In your salaried job, you may have earned $50,000 annually but you worked long daily hours, weekends, holidays and were forever problem-solving and thinking about the job. Factor into the equation the additional time spent carrying out your responsibilities, then figure the hourly rate for an annual salary. You may be shocked to discover that you were actually working for a minimal wage all that time.

6. Weekly paychecks. A fluctuating income can be scary if you have always been salaried, but a weekly paycheck makes it easy to keep track of expenses. When I first started temping, I laid out expenses for the month on a week-by-week basis. I knew how many hours I needed to work to pay my bills. It was easy to tell if I was earning enough to pay expenses.

Expenses for May 1994 (example)

Week of 5/6		Week of 5/13	
Rent	$600.00	Car	$200.00
Electric	46.23	Visa	45.63
Parking	30.00	Telephone	32.00
Haircut	30.00	Medical ins.	200.00

(Week of 5/6: I had better clear $800)
(Week of 5/13: I had better clear $600)

So, how much money *can* you make?

The truth is, you'll never become a millionaire from what you'll make as a temp. But you can make a respectable living at it. Of course, the more specialized your skills (computer software knowledge, for example), the higher your pay.

Temps are paid at an hourly rate, receiving overtime pay for work over 40 hours a week. According to Bruce Steinberg at the National Association of Temporary Services, several factors determine the size of hourly rate: seasonal (accountants will earn more in April than they will in July); regional, and supply and demand. For instance, word processors in New York City may not receive more money than those in St. Louis in spite of higher regional wages. New York City has a surplus, St. Louis does not. What is the dollar range? In theory, from minimum wage for unskilled labor to several hundred dollars per hour for an interim CEO.

So, at $8 per hour, a 40-hour week (at 48 weeks per year, allowing four weeks for holidays, vacation, illness) will bring in $15,360. If you work a 45-hour week (8:30 a.m. to 6 p.m., a half-hour for lunch), earning five hours of time-and-a-half each week, it jumps to $18,240.

At $14 per hour, 40-hour weeks give you $26,880 and 45-hour weeks produce $31,920 yearly.

The chart below shows common hourly rates (New York City) for general office workers with typing ($8 to $12) and computer word processing ($12 to $18). The salaries are based on 48 weeks per year, allowing four weeks for holidays, vacation or illness. One group is for a 45-hour week, which encompasses five hours of time-and-a-half pay each week; the other is for a basic 9-to-5, one-hour-for-lunch, 35-hour week.

Rate Hourly	45-Hour-Week			35-Hour-Week		
	Daily	Weekly	Yearly	Daily	Weekly	Yearly
$10	$90	$475	$22,800	$70	$350	$16,800
$14	$126	$665	$31,920	$98	$490	$23,520
$18	$162	$855	$41,040	$126	$630	$30,240

A truer picture of potential income is given when the allowable business deductions are taken, adding anywhere from $5,000 to $10,000 more real income to the annual base. Deductions and tax information are covered in Chapter 9.

Start-up costs

Organization, as always, is crucial to the successful juggling of multiple tasks. There are two items that will be great help to you: a telephone-answering machine and an organizer. Theoretically, you can function without these items, but why make it harder for yourself? Tips follow on how to select the best ones for the job.

Telephone-answering machines

The answering machine becomes your lifeline to the outside world when your "work" number is constantly changing. Selecting the right machine for yourself becomes especially important when it is used as a business tool. You might want to consider some of these factors when you buy one.

Common Job Categories, Descriptions and Hourly Rates Used By New York City Agencies

Category	Description	Hourly Rate
General Clerk	Filing, sorting, collating	$5 - $6
Mailroom Aide	Self-Explanatory	$5 - $6
Proxy Clerk	Self-Explanatory, depending on experience	$5 - $8
Figure Clerk	Affinity for figures, can function as order-processing clerk, payroll clerk.	$6 - $8
CRT Operator	Heavy alpha and numeric	$6 - $9
Receptionist	Meet & greet, accept & route packages take messages, "front office" appearance.	$8
Reception/Typist	Same as above along with typing 35/40 words per minute.	
Switchboard Operator - One Position Board	Ability to handle high volume of incoming calls.	$8 - $9
Guy/Gal Friday Secretary (General)	Excellent clerical skill with good telephone, manner, typing 45/50. Can use transcription equipment, schedule appointments, make travel arrangements. Use fast longhand, speedwriting, etc.	$10 - $11
Secretary (Executive)	All of above, but can also function as "right hand" to executive.	$12 - $13
Word-Processing Secretary	All of above, but with word processing.	$13 - $16
Word-Processing Operator	Essentially a production person. Can function with minimum supervision for word-processing center. No secretarial duties.	$14 - $17

Rate Ranges

Proofreaders: $8 - $15; Trainers: $25 - $60; Copywriters: $15 - $30; Technical Writers: $18 - $40. Note: Legal Secretaries, Word Processors and Proofreaders get slightly higher rates.

1. How is the quality of the sound? Will your message sound like a disembodied voice from outer space?

2. Answering machines that use one tape for both outgoing and incoming messages have very long beeps if there are messages waiting. Callers often think the machine is broken.

3. Does the machine have the capacity to record the number of messages you expect to receive?

4. "Toll-saver" feature will save on long-distance charges by letting you know if you have any new messages since you last called to retrieve.

5. "Auto erase" from another location is a helpful feature, allowing you to erase the messages you have already heard before returning home.

6. "Outbound message change" from another telephone is also useful if you want to record a different message.

Some agencies furnish beepers for their temps; some temps carry beepers of their own, especially if they are available for evening work. Beepers are an option, not a necessity.

Organizer/planners

I also recommend purchasing some form of portable pocket calendar/organizer to keep track of your schedule. In selecting a commercial organizer/planner, keep the following points in mind:

1. **Size and weight.** You will be carrying it with you daily.

2. **Flexibility.** Can you adapt it to your needs? If there are too many sections that do not apply to you, you can take them out, but will you have to pay for them? Will you be able to add other sections in the future?

3. **Design.** Are the to-do sheets or other forms designed in a way that you would use?

4. **Pockets.** Are there places to carry bank deposit slips, stamps or stash business receipts?

5. **Appearance.** Does it look professional for the image you want to project? Of course if it doesn't suit your needs, and you don't use it, it doesn't matter how professional it looks.

Most people start temping as I did, by accident, then go on to figure out how to do it well by learning from their mistakes. You have the advantage of reading a book that will get you started on the right foot from the very beginning. Give it a try. Temping is relatively risk-free. The worst that can happen is that you'll have a few humorous escapades to talk about at parties.

Chapter 2

Getting Started: Finding, Evaluating and Registering With a Temporary Agency

The easiest and quickest way to get work is to register with a temporary employment company. Although they are usually called "agencies," that is a somewhat misleading term. These companies are considered the *employers* of people who work as temporary employees (temps). They provide a service—they find temporary employees to fulfill the work needs of their client companies. As employers, they are subject to the same state regulation as other companies: They must provide unemployment insurance, disability insurance and worker's compensation. The employees (temps) are covered under the regulations provided by their states and, as such, are entitled to plan benefits.

The agency/temp relationship

Agencies employ temps to work for their clients—thus, temps are employees of the agency. However, "employee" does not adequately represent those professional temps who manage their temporary work as small businesses. The relationship is much more synergistic. In

27

these instances, agencies function in a manner closely akin to *bookers*; they "sell" a temp's time and talent, then take a "commission" (a portion of the hourly rate charged to clients). Unlike professional bookers, agencies do not actively market an individual temp's services. Professional temps use several "booking" agencies and are the managers of these multiple relationships.

Over the years, temporary employment agencies have not always enjoyed a particularly good reputation or good press. Some of it was justly earned, some not. How do fledgling temps find good agencies to represent them? What if those stories you may have heard regarding unethical agencies are true? How does one assess an agency during the interview process?

How to find agencies

The most effective way to find a good agency is to talk to other temps: people who have worked as temps in the past, or temps presently working in your office. Ask which agencies they like to work for, and why. Find out what they *don't* like about various agencies. Most temps are quite willing to share information. Talk to temps you consider incompetent or obnoxious. Find out where they work and be cautious about registering at these places.

In addition, read the classified ads in the daily papers, especially the weekend editions. Agencies advertise for the skills they need. When they advertise for word processors, they list the software packages they want. Agencies also advertise in specialty papers, such as those geared to attorneys and performers. Take a look at newspapers or newsletters targeted to your particular profession. Your local library is a good place to do this. Librarians can steer you to papers you may not know about.

In New York City, for example, temp agencies advertise heavily in *The New York Times, New York Law Journal* (found in most law offices) and *Back Stage* (a weekly newspaper for performers).

The telephone directory yellow pages, under "Employment Contractors: Temporary Help" lists temporary agencies. Many agencies buy display ads that give information about their specialties as well as their location.

Often, agencies congregate in one or two office buildings conveniently located to many of the clients they serve. Finding out where the agencies are clustered allows you to make a more efficient use of your time when you register, and later on when you are delivering timesheets or picking up paychecks.

Specialty agencies

Doctors, medical professionals, lawyers, paralegals, accountants, scientists, pharmacists, childcare workers, computer industry professionals and business management professionals. Whatever your profession, chances are that there's a temporary agency that specializes in placing individuals in your field.

Professional membership organizations may be a good source for referrals to such agencies. Some organizations maintain employment hotlines and job banks. For instance, the National Writers Union maintains two job banks—one for technical writers and one for general writing assignments.

While there are agencies representing most professions, it is difficult to maintain current information. Names and addresses change, agencies may merge with others under combined names or go out of business altogether. Libraries have association directories that are updated yearly. One you may want to check out is the *National and Professional Associations in the United States*. Another is the *Encyclopedia of Associations*. Also, Executive Recruiter News publishes the *Directory of Temporary Firms*.

Registering to work

Looking polished, poised and professional will get you considered for the better jobs. To begin, select five agencies either by the recommendations of others, or their proximity to each other. Get yourself organized and dressed for success (in their eyes, that is) and start registering.

Attire. Look your most mainstream corporate. This is not the day to have clothing display your individuality.

- **Men:** Wear a dark suit and tie. If you don't have a suit, wear a sport coat and slacks, or a dark sweater with a shirt underneath it, and slacks. Armani silks and "Miami Vice" stubble are not a good idea.

- **Women:** Wear a dark suit, stockings and conservative heels. Keep jewelry, makeup and perfume to a minimum. Save your high-fashion ensembles for another occasion.

Organization. You want to impress upon the temporary agency that you are a reliable, efficient and productive worker. It's crucial, then, that during your first interview with the agency that you communicate this by being well-prepared. You don't want to seem flustered, forgetful, disorganized or appear as a novice. Be sure to take with you:

- Several copies of resumes or a personal data fact sheet (see page 32).
- *Two* acceptable forms of identification to prove you are a citizen. Agencies will accept *two* of the following: a driver's license, a Social Security card, a birth certificate or a passport. Noncitizens will need to show their work visas.
- Your list of references, with addresses and telephone numbers. If another temp referred you to the agency, have his or her name handy and mention it. (Better yet, ask the temp to make an "introductory" telephone call in your behalf.)

The resume. Don't make the mistake of "downgrading" your resume by deemphasizing or leaving off much of your experience and achievements; being "overqualified" helps more than it hinders. If you decide to rewrite your present resume, you might want to emphasize your administrative skills, and highlight your computer knowledge and software packages, if appropriate.

If you don't have a resume, compile a "Personal Data Fact Sheet," which will answer most commonly asked questions about your education, your service record and references. The sample on page 32 was dreamed up by Frank Joerss during his period of unemployment. He disliked filling out applications, so he came up with this alternative. (I have adapted Frank's form by removing his personal information and substituting phony data.)

What to expect

While you don't necessarily need an appointment, it is wise to inquire ahead of time what the hours are for interviewing/testing and which day is pay day. Pay days are hectic; avoid registering then unless you want to take a look at other temps employed by that agency.

For the most part, the registration process is not a wonderful experience. The receptionist will hand you forms to complete and, in many agencies, will administer any tests that you take. A counselor (also called work coordinator or service coordinator) will interview you afterward. Counselors/coordinators are staff employees who assign temps to the job orders received by agencies. The terms are used interchangeably in this book.

If you have no keyboard skills, and even less interest in secretarial work, the majority of agencies will still insist on a typing test. In far too many places, the test is executed on a decrepit typewriter with loose keys and loud rattles, perched on a rickety typing stand—and located in the noisiest area of the office.

Often, even if you have word-processing and/or computer skills, the decrepit typewriter is still the testing machine of choice, and the person testing you may not have any knowledge that computer and word processor keyboards are different. Just get the test out of the way, doing the best you can under the circumstances.

Most agencies administer grammar, vocabulary and spelling tests. Some give a simple arithmetic test. Examples of these tests are included at the end of the chapter.

For those people with computer skills, almost all agencies will test you on at least one of the software packages you claim to know. More and more agencies are using "hands-on" tests. A popular series is "Qwiz."

If, however, the agency gives a written test, the chances are good it will stress some of the software's more obscure functions. Chances are even better that all computer tests will be administered by someone who will boast proudly at some point, "I don't know anything about computers." Don't lose heart.

I made quick reference sheets for all of my software. When you know 20 different programs, you don't have the keystrokes of every software package fresh in your memory at all times. Also, many people use templates and are used to looking at the template rather than memorizing keystrokes. I used the reference sheets during tests, and no one ever said anything. A WordPerfect quick reference sheet is included at the end of the chapter as an example of what I'm talking about.

Personal Data Fact Sheet

This fact sheet is being submitted, along with my resume, in lieu of any standard employment application required.

Name:	Barker, Susan Mary
Address:	1188 Hastings Avenue, La Mesa, CA 94102
Telephone:	(619) 948-5773
Social Security #:	503-80-6034

Citizen of U.S.?	Yes
Ever been convicted of a crime?	No
Under age 18?	No
Military service?	None

Education

Name of school	Address	Degree	Major study
San Diego State University	San Diego, CA	B.A.	Sociology Minors: Poli. Sci/ Psychology

Computers/software IBM Environment

Word Processing	**Spreadsheets**
WordPerfect	Lotus 1-2-3
Microsoft Word	EXCEL
Multimate	

Employment history (For responsibilities, please see resume.)

1. DTA Automation Consulting
   121 Granda Crest
   White Plains, NY 10603
   (914) 946-3507

   From: 1985-Present
   Job Title: Administrator
   Reported to: D. Thrailkill, V.P.
   Reason for leaving: Downsizing

References

1. Lonnie Solin, VP Marketing, Regency Premiums (212) 867-5034
2. Elaine Rokow, SVP Lending, Morgan Stanley (212) 867-0005

Representative questions for both word-processing and spreadsheet tests are listed at the end of the chapter. If you can perform the functions listed on these tests, you will have no trouble passing.

If you are a beginning word processor, you can purchase easily portable templates and reference products at software stores. The templates will have keystrokes for a particular software package in a format that fits onto the keyboard. Some of them have "mini-manuals" attached, such as those, below, manufactured by TDA, Inc., 800-624-2101.

Increase your marketability

Temporary agencies (and this economy) are more interested in your skill base than your former title. Try to think about your business attributes in a less traditional way. The more skills you can list—from volunteer work, hobbies, community service—the more opportunities are open to you. Here are a few simple examples that will get you started.

You will be more marketable if you perform decently on the typing test. Light typing may be part of a research job (labels, envelopes, short memos) that would pay a higher rate and may lead to other opportunities within the company.

Take a "fast longhand" test on the dictaphone for the same reasons: marketability and more money. You can probably scribble at 30 words per minute the immortal rambling of the dinosaur who still dictates. (Transcribe immediately afterwards while your memory is fresh and you can decipher the scribbles.)

Many agencies have some form of "legal knowledge" test. I had no trouble passing these tests when I first began temping. I have served on school boards in California and New York (education law). I have sued a major corporation (litigation). I have even filled in as a para-legal on occasion.

Are you good at detail work? Do you know proofreader's symbols? Many agencies give proofreader's tests.

What skills do you use pursuing your hobbies? Photography? Graphic design? Amateur collectors may find work in museums and galleries, perhaps assisting in the indexing of an inventory as a start.

Register with several agencies

Don't forget that you are the small business owner of your time, talent and skill; the agencies are your bookers. Registering with more than one of them is especially important in a slow economy. No single agency will keep you busy with choice assignments every day, even in the best of times. If you register with only one booker, you'll have all the problems of a single employer with few of the benefits. Register with four to five. It is a manageable number while learning the ropes, and significantly increases your chances of employment. Managing these multiple agency relationships is further detailed in Chapter 4.

Prepare for the interview by thinking through your answers to the questions that follow, and rehearsing, if necessary, until you feel comfortable with your answers If interviewing and testing throw you into a panic, take a field trip to whichever agency is said to be the "worst" (and that you have no interest in working for) and register. Subsequent interviews will only get better. The object of this exercise is to get practice playing the interview game.

Questions agencies will ask you

Besides the usual interview questions about present skills and former employment, agencies may ask the questions listed here:

1. Why do you want to do temporary work?

If you have never worked as a temp before, someone is going to ask you that at one point or another. Agencies will have little interest in investing much time or effort in placing someone who may only work for a few weeks until landing a job. Job-seekers looking for full-time work might want to stress their lack of urgency while investigating numerous opportunities before making a decision, perhaps taking as long as a year to look around at what's out there.

2. Do you have any scheduling restrictions?

Obviously, the more flexibility you have, the more marketable you are—especially if you can work evenings and weekends. At the very least, do everything you can to be available during the core work hours of 9 to 5—make childcare arrangements, check the bus schedules, etc. Don't give the interviewer complex restrictions like, "I can only work from 10:00 a.m. until 2:30 p.m. Mondays and Wednesdays, and on Tuesdays and Thursdays, I have to leave before noon." You'll only limit—or eliminate—placement opportunities.

Of course, if you do have scheduling restrictions that you can't change—for example, you can't work on Wednesdays—be up front about it.

3. Is there any kind of work you won't do?

Keep an open mind—it makes you more marketable. You really can't judge the work until you get on the job. At this point, it's pointless to limit your options. However, if there's something you *can't* do because of physical limitations (a bad back, allergies to some products), it's wise to mention it.

4. What hourly rate are you looking for?

Give the rate range for your skill. Ask, if you don't know what it is—or, better yet, make sure you've done your research before the interview, so you know what the going rate is for your skills. Consider taking a low rate to establish yourself with the agency, especially if you haven't worked before as a temp. Think of it as a subsidized apprenticeship.

5. What form of transportation will you use?

You might want to consider *not* sharing information about your elaborate arrangements to get to the train station or to borrow a car.

Just assure the interviewer that transportation to any job site is not a problem for you.

Questions to ask agencies when you register

Yes, *you* have a right to ask questions, too. Consider this a two-way interview. None of the following questions is impertinent or out of order. If the interviewer is evasive or reluctant to answer, you might want to reconsider working at that particular agency.

1. What are your business hours? Do you use an answering service/answering machine after hours? How frequently are the messages checked? Do you use call-forwarding?

   This information is especially important when you must reach the agency in an emergency. Rare is the life without an occasional crisis; almost as rare as the emergency that occurs during normal business hours.

2. When must timesheets be in? What day of the week is pay day? Is the check from a local bank? Are there convenient check-cashing arrangements? Are you open late on pay day? Can timesheets be faxed, hours called in, paychecks delivered?

   If the agency closes daily at 5:30 p.m., without exception, you need to know that there are arrangements to get your paycheck if you don't finish working until 6. If your assignment is located at some distance from the agency, it will be helpful if they let you call in your hours, or fax the timesheet to them. When agencies have a large number of temps at one location, they will often deliver the paychecks.

3. What are some of the industries you serve? Who are some of your client companies?

   If you have an intense dislike for attorneys, and law firms make up 90 percent of their client base, this may not be the right agency for you.

4. What is the range of your pay rates for first, second and third shifts? At what point do you give merit or seniority increases in hourly rates? In a month? A year? Never? What are your weekend and holiday rates?

   Do they give you straight answers to these questions? Take notes on any information you get regarding their rates and the frequency of their increases.

5. How does overtime work? Are there different rates for evening and late shift? Are the rates for weekend work higher?

   Before asking about overtime, please read carefully the information about how to figure it correctly in Chapter 9. Unfortunately, not all agencies give the correct information to their temps, sometimes through ignorance, other times deliberately. The purpose of asking the question is to alert you to the potential future problems, not to get into an argument if the response is incorrect.

6. Do you have medical or dental benefits?

   Most agencies have descriptive brochures about their plans. Don't be surprised to find so many restrictions that the benefits are virtually useless to you (to be eligible for coverage, no breaks in employment—or a required number of monthly hours).

7. Do you offer vacation pay? Training?

   The restrictions on vacations may be similar to medical and dental benefits. Just make sure you understand the policy ahead of time, if vacations are important to you.

   Having a place to learn and practice a new software package, or to swap information with another temp is invaluable. Some agencies will even pay a trainer to teach temps they feel are worth the investment.

8. Do you have referral bonuses?

   Some agencies encourage such referrals: Refer a friend and get anywhere from $25 to $100 when they work 50 to 100 hours for the agency.

9. Do you have a temp lounge or a place where I can stand by? May I use your telephone when I stand by?

10. What is your policy if I accept a permanent job from a client?

    Agencies are prohibited by law from charging a permanent placement fee. Instead, they are permitted "liquidated damages" equal to a percentage of the annual salary of the person placed. Another case of a rose by another name. Most agencies call it a "finder's fee." Usually the terms of their contract with you and clients are spelled out on the back of the timesheets.

    Everything is negotiable. Waiving finder's fees from a good client is not unusual. On one job where I ended up taking a consulting project, my agreement with the agency was to use the agency's temps first, provided they could provide me with the skills I needed. If they couldn't, I would go elsewhere. The project lasted nine months. The agency earned much goodwill from the client, and made considerably more money doing it this way than by taking a fee for "liquidated damages."

11. Is the agency a member of the National Association of Temporary Services (NATS) or a state association?

NATS is a national trade association that furnishes legal, legislative and regulatory information to its members. Members subscribe to a code of ethics. While it implies a certain level of professionalism, it's no guarantee of a good service. If the agency is not a member of any association, you might inquire why.

12. Ask counselors interviewing you how long they have been with the agency and what they like best about working there. As a whole, the industry has a lot of turnover. Answers to these questions will give you some idea of the depth of the counselor's industry or agency knowledge.

Because of the time needed for testing and interviewing, you can register with approximately three agencies in a day. However, there is a new service in New York City called Baseline Recruiters Network, Inc., that I think will revolutionize the registration process. Temps who register at Baseline have their applications distributed electronically to dozens of temporary services (and employment agencies) that subscribe to the Baseline database. The temp's resume information and skill rating is matched against the subscriber orders every night for three months. They charge a small fee to the temp as well as to their subscribers. Think of the time saved by completing basic information and testing once for multiple registrations!

Persistence pays

Most people new to temporary employment register with an agency, then sit back and wait for the telephone to ring. A common complaint is "I was never called for any work."

To increase the odds that the agency will place you, you must call and give agencies your availability *daily* until you are working. Then, you call to let them know your work telephone number and when you will be available again. These are quick calls. For instance, on Monday morning:

> *"Hi, this is Fred Watkins. I'm looking for work for today and the rest of the week. I can be reached at home."*

Alas, you don't get work. Call again in the afternoon.

> *"Hi, this is Fred Watkins again. I'm still looking for work. For tomorrow and the rest of the week. I can be reached at home."*

Not a good sign

Some agencies proudly tell clients and applicants that they give morning wake-up calls to their temps. Other agencies call without warning, causing chest pains for those of us who only receive emergency calls at 6 a.m. I allow the agency one mistake with this. I do not wish to work for an agency that employs people who can't get themselves out of bed in the morning.

I tell the caller, pleasantly and firmly, that I neither need nor want a wake-up call. I do not growl; he or she is just following instructions. Later in the morning I call the counselor I work with and convey the same message. Sometimes I mention, jokingly of course, that I get up at 5 a.m. and might be inspired to give their staff a call or two to get them up and running for the day.

If the "vibes" aren't right during the registration process, take heed. The agency is probably putting its best foot forward to interest you in working for them. This is the courtship stage. This is as good as it gets.

You can't judge an agency by office ambiance, but you can by the behavior of its personnel. Some offices are tacky at best, but the jobs are good and the people are pros. The overworked receptionist will treat applicants courteously while fielding calls in a business-like manner. There is never any reason to work for rude or patronizing people. There are too many fine agencies to choose from.

Temp By Choice

MATH SKILLS EVALUATION

Time: 15 minutes

Add:

```
 2    3/4          3,6078.34              35 + 18 + 54 + 87 =
12    1/2          8,7089.01
 7    3/8            901.56               43.2 + 76.32 + 2.1 =
14    1/4          2,3234.01
```

Subtract:

```
70,695      435.40      12,897.43      665.21
10,243       23.43       6,909.54      458.98
```

Multiply:

```
34567       5467.87      3 x 4 x 12 =      3/4 x 2/3 =
   12           .23      1/2 x 14   =
```

3 cases of bolts @ $2.95 per case =

80 acres of land @ $1,908 per acre =

Divide:

```
432 ) 8796              6.09) 761.54
```

Percentage:

15 is what percent of 75?

What percent of 200 is 10?

SPELLING EVALUATION

Please circle the correct spelling.

1.	article	artical	articale	artacle
2.	necesary	necessary	necessery	neccesary
3.	acomodate	accomodate	accommodate	acommodate
4.	knowlige	knowledge	knowlage	knowlege
5.	emphasise	emphasize	emphesize	emphesise
6.	injustice	injustise	enjustice	injustece
7.	privilage	privelige	privilege	priviledge
8.	momentum	mommentum	momuntem	momentim

Spreadsheet Test

If you can perform the following functions, you will pass many spreadsheet tests without much trouble.

1. Call up the program.
2. Retrieve and/or create spreadsheet.
3. Label a specific cell location.
4. Place a value in a specific cell location.
5. Center align the label to a column using a command.
6. Insert a row.
7. Delete a column.
8. Move a range of data to another location.
9. Copy a range of data to another location.
10. Use "GOTO."
11. Using edit command function, change center-aligned label and data.
12. Name a range.
13. Change cell width of a column.
14. Format to show commas, but no decimal places.
15. Insert a page break.
16. Call up "Help" screen for data commands.
17. Using appropriate function, display the sum of a column in a specific location.
18. Save a file.
19. Print.
20. Create and view a bar chart showing Temporary Sales for the last two years of data. Show years on X-axis.
21. Display average sales for 1994 figures in one column.
22. Sort is ascending order using designated column as primary key.
23. Exit.

Word Processing Test

If you can perform the following functions, you will pass most word-processing tests with flying colors.

1. From the subdirectory prompt, enter the command to load the program.
2. Retrieve a document.
3. Change the left/right and top/bottom margins.
4. Change the line spacing to double space.
5. Center the date.
6. Insert two words in a sentence.
7. Delete four words.
8. Cut and move a paragraph to another location.
9. Copy and place another paragraph in a different location.
10. Save and exit the document without exiting the program.
11. Use the print menu to print two copies.
12. Indent a paragraph.
13. Enter underlined text, underlining as you type.
14. Enter boldfaced text, bolding as you type.
15. Hard page break.
16. Use "GOTO."
17. Use subscript.
18. Call up the "Help" screen.
19. Search and replace a word.
20. Merge two fields.
21. In a 70-column screen, clear all tabs then establish new left-aligned at 1.5", 3.5", 5.5" and 7.5".
22. Use decimal tabs to line up:

$$123.12$$
$$1234.12$$
$$12345.12$$

23. Create a new document.
24. Exit word processing without saving document

WordPerfect 5.1 Template (Enhanced Layout)

```
Ö¿¿¿¿¿F1¿¿¿¿¿¿¿¿¿ÒF2¿¿¿¿¿¿¿¿¿F3¿¿¿¿¿¿¿¿¿¿F4¿¿¿¿¿¿¿¿Ò¿           Legend:
 °  Shell     °   Spell    °   Screen      °   Move      °   Ctrl + Function Key
 °  Thesaurus °   Replace  °  °Reveal Codes °   Block     °   Alt  + Function Key
 °  SETUP     °   <-SEARCH °   SWITCH      °  ->INDENT<-  °   SHIFT + FUNCTION KEY
 °  Cancel    °   ->Search °   Help        °  ->Indent    °   Function Key alone
 À¿¿¿¿¿¿¿¿¿¿¿¿¿¿¿¿¿¿¿¿¿¿¿¿¿¿¿¿¿¿¿¿¿¿¿¿¿¿¿Ù

 Ö¿¿¿¿¿¿F5¿¿¿¿¿¿¿¿¿ÒF6¿¿¿¿¿¿¿¿¿F7¿¿¿¿¿¿¿¿Ò¿¿¿¿F8¿¿¿¿Ò¿
 °  Text In/Out °  Tab Align  °  Footnote   °   Font       °
 °  Mark Text   °  Flush Right °  Columns/Table° Style      °
 ° DATE/OUTLINE °  CENTER     °   PRINT      °   FORMAT     °
 °  List        °  Bold       °   Exit       °   Underline  °
 À¿¿¿¿¿¿¿¿¿¿¿¿¿¿¿¿¿¿¿¿¿¿¿¿¿¿¿¿¿¿¿¿¿¿¿¿¿¿¿Ù

 Ö¿¿¿¿¿¿F9¿¿¿¿¿¿¿¿¿ÒF10¿¿¿¿¿¿¿¿¿F11¿¿¿¿¿¿¿¿F12¿¿¿¿¿¿Ò¿
 °  Merge/Sort  ° Macro Define °                °          °
 °  Graphics    °   Macro      °                °          °
 °  MERGE CODES °   RETRIEVE   °                °          °
 °  End Field   °   Save       °  °Reveal Codes °  Block    °
 À¿¿¿¿¿¿¿¿¿¿¿¿¿¿¿¿¿¿¿¿¿¿¿¿¿¿¿¿¿¿¿¿¿¿¿¿¿¿¿Ù
```

Press 1 to view the PC/XT keyboard template

(Press ENTER to exit Help)

Selection: 0

Chapter 3

Handling Your First Assignments Like a Pro

....

Now that you've successfully registered at several agencies, your next step is to handle your first assignments in a professional manner, thus establishing yourself as a dependable and competent temporary employee. When that first call comes, the counselor will say something like, "I have work for you for tomorrow. An admin/assist spot for the day, using WordPerfect and light Lotus."

Your lines in this little vignette are, "Tell me more about the position." Then you ask the questions that reflect your concerns about the work.

"Is it a busy spot? Are there heavy telephones?"

"What kind of work will I do most of the day?"

As you listen to your new job description, keep an open mind. Realize that the counselor is merely repeating what someone from that company's personnel department said *after* a manager described the position initially. By the time you hear the job description, it may not be accurate. If the counselor doesn't have answers to your questions ("Do they need someone with strong graphics skills? I'm pretty slow."), he or she can call the client to find out. It is in everyone's best interests to place the right temp in the job.

Questions to ask your counselor about the job

1. What kind of work does the job entail? If it's word processing, what machine or software experience do they want?

   If there are any tasks you loathe, now is the time to find out if the job includes them, and for what percent of the day. (Data entry? Heavy telephones? Dictaphone? Proofreading?)

2. What is the assignment length? What are the daily hours? Is overtime expected?

3. What is the company name, the address (including floor) and the name of the person I report to?

4. What are the directions, names of cross streets, and available public transportation to the job site?

5. What is the company's smoking policy?

   Smokers will need to know if they can smoke at their desk, in a lounge, outside the building, etc. Nonsmokers may want to know if they are in a smoke-free environment.

6. Are there any job requirements that may conflict with my physical limitations?

   Although you've already discussed such problems with the agency in your initial interview, it's wise to bring up any physical limitations again at this point. I no longer take heavy word-processing jobs because of my carpal-tunnel condition, so that's something I always ask about. Someone with a broken foot and limited mobility would inquire about building access and stairs.

7. What is the hourly rate?

Usually, rate is not discussed until it is determined that you are able to do the job and want to. When you are first starting out, I advise you to take what is offered rather than to negotiate for the highest salary. You need to prove yourself to the agency. Once your reputation is established, you can negotiate a better rate.

Declining assignments

I try to accept most assignments, as I have learned the job description can often be misleading. When you are starting out, it's a good idea to accept as many assignments as possible, to establish with the agency that they can count on you. However, when you feel you must decline an assignment, tell the counselor pleasantly, "I don't think I'm the right person for this job, but thanks for thinking of me. Please keep me in mind for something else." Counselors are well aware that neither jobs nor temps come in "one size fits all."

When the company requests an interview

If the assignment is a long-term one, it is in your best interest to meet the people and to take a look at the work environment. You and the prospective employer can determine if it would be a good match, and it gives you a better feel about whether to commit for a period of time. I don't interview for assignments shorter than one month.

This meeting should be a chance for you and your prospective employer to meet each other to determine whether this would be a good match. You shouldn't have to undergo more tests, though. This is duplicating the agency's work and wasting your time. If I wanted to engage in those unpaid activities, I would spend my time applying for permanent jobs.

As a rule, you can schedule these company interviews either before or after regular work hours.

Job information

Working for several agencies in a variety of jobs means juggling information. I designed an assignment form to record the job particulars and to remind me what I need to ask about. (See the sample on the next page.) It is easy to carry in a pocket or bag for quick reference.

Assignment Form

Company _____

_____

Address _____

_____

Floor _____
Ask For _____

_____

Agency _____
Rate _____
How Long _____
Hours _____
Machine _____
Software _____

_____

Duties _____

_____

_____

_____

_____

Directions _____

_____

_____

_____

_____

_____

_____

When I arrive at the assignment, I also make a note of the information on my calendar/organizer, adding the time I arrive and the telephone number of the workstation I occupy. I jot down my times for lunch, and the time I leave. This is the same information recorded on the timesheet, but I usually toss my copy once I receive the corresponding paycheck. Keeping it in my calendar/organizer gives me a convenient record of the work and rate if there is any discrepancy on my paycheck. Also, if I leave behind any personal belongings, I don't have to involve the agency in their retrieval.

First impressions

As you begin your first day on your new temp job, keep professional demeanor uppermost in your mind at all times. That's what sets you apart, often from the full-time employees. Indeed, it calms, as well, the apprehensions of those who look askance at temps.

I recommend arriving 15 minutes early on the first day. Many times, companies are afraid "the temp won't show" and your early arrival allays these fears. You are paid for the time. Be sure to include it on your timesheet. Never have I not been paid for this time.

Shake hands when you meet *anyone* at the new company—from the receptionist to your supervisor. Those who find temps weird will be relieved that you know their ways.

Shortly after you arrive at the assignment, call your agency to give your telephone number or extension. As a matter of courtesy, tell your supervisor that you must make the call, so it won't be perceived that you walked in and started calling friends. (At that time, I let the supervisor know I will be calling my daughter as well to give her my number.)

From time to time, you might be left waiting for 15 minutes to a half-hour in the reception area, until someone in personnel has time to take you to the workstation. This is especially true at large companies. Ask the receptionist if you may call the agency from a courtesy telephone to let them know of your arrival. (I have never been refused. When there isn't a courtesy telephone, the receptionist has called for me.) You can call again later with your telephone number. You are paid for the waiting time.

Relay the workstation number to your other agencies. When you expect to work longer than one day, you can call agencies over the course of the assignment. If the assignment is for only one day and you must find work for the remainder of the week, make sure you talk to all of your counselors. It is acceptable to call agencies from the job; it is, after all, your livelihood.

Sometimes you may be without a convenient telephone. Tell your supervisor you must call agencies and ask for a telephone to use during a lunch break. Rarely have I had to do this, but no one has ever refused my request. (Agencies will relay messages to you through the personnel department if you don't have a direct line.)

If the company's telephone calls come through a receptionist, call reception to give your name, location and extension. You don't want to run the risk of missing future job assignments because the receptionist never heard of you and swore you didn't work there.

Even when everyone has your work number, continue to check your answering machine messages at least hourly. Counselors can misplace scraps of paper with telephone numbers written on them.

At the end of the shift, make it a point to say good-bye to people and thank them for the courtesies extended to you, if appropriate. You always want to leave on a good note, even if the assignment wasn't a good one for you or the company one you'd want to work for again. The company is a client of your temporary agency, and the work there will pay someone else's rent.

The work environment

In the ideal situation, your work will have been planned, someone will be assigned to introduce you to co-workers and show you where the lavatories and kitchen are, the desk or office where you sit will have the supplies you need and the telephone list/book will be handy. There will be a one-page instruction sheet about the office routine.

In the ideal situation.

Although 99 percent of the time you will work in clean, safe and comfortable surroundings, once in a while you will find a company that thinks employees in general, and temps in particular, can work in airless chambers perched on rickety chairs at makeshift desks. Don't hesitate to ask for whatever you need to make the quarters habitable, including a move to a different location. In addition, you need a safe place to store your purse if you carry one. I am reasonable and gracious about these demands, but firm.

Temps who are requested to work past 8 p.m. are usually sent home in a taxi if they work in a metropolitan area and use public transportation. You might want to inquire what the company policy is before agreeing to work late.

On occasion, you will have to share a work area or equipment. Most of the time, people are considerate and this works out fine. If the environment is intolerable, and you are unable to rectify the situation tactfully, tell the agency. Perhaps a counselor can work out a solution, or get you moved to a different location. If not, tough out the day. Ask for a replacement. Don't return to the company.

Sometimes you are taken to your workstation by an employee from personnel who doesn't know much about the job. In these instances you will be given little or no useful information about the position. Even when people are knowledgeable, you won't always be given the information you need to do a good job. "Regular" employees forget that you don't know their company procedures. You have to know what questions to ask.

The three most important questions

1. Whom do I work for? Get names, locations and telephone numbers. A harried employee can drop you off at a vacant desk, muttering vague instructions, before rushing off to his or her next crisis and leaving you uncertain who your supervisor is.

2. Who will answer my questions? Don't assume that other department members will have information you need, or that they'll want to be bothered. Get a designated question-answerer.

3. Which telephone number is mine and how does the system work? Find out the correct prefix if there is a direct line. Don't assume you can be reached by 592-8132 because 592-8000 is the general number. Direct lines can be, and often are, a different prefix.

More important questions

The questions that follow will need to be asked at some point during the day. Don't walk in and begin an interrogation—or they will *know* you are weird.

1. Whose telephones should I answer? What would you like me to say?

2. Who are my co-workers? (Get a telephone list for the department as well as an internal telephone directory.)

3. Will I need a special card or number combination to enter and leave the building, use the lavatories, or use the copier and fax machine?

    Law firms are frequent users of temporary help. The first time you work for one (or an accounting firm), you will find that the professionals have billable hours. They use task logs to keep records of work done for clients. Their record-keeping includes attorney (or accountant) numbers, client numbers and matter numbers. To operate the telephone, fax or copy machines, you need to key in these numbers. The numbers are also needed to request a messenger or to send mail. Professional temps know to ask for these numbers immediately, and to get a back-up administrative code in case a number is inoperable.

4. What is the name of the messenger service? (It is seldom listed on the rolodex under "M" for messenger.)

5. Will forms or account numbers be needed to use the service?

6. What is the number for technical support or the LAN administrator (if you are using the computer or on a local area network)?

7. Am I supposed to cover for anyone at lunch?

    (Sometimes in busy areas everyone—managers included—pitches in to cover the telephones.)

8. How is the mail handled? Will I be expected to pick it up from the mail room? Is there mail coming to me that I should open or handle in some way? When is the last pickup of the day?

9. Which courier service do I use? Where are the forms and envelopes kept? When is the last pickup of the day?

10. Who signs the timesheet at the end of the day?

    (Some companies have temps report back to personnel. People leave early on Fridays, and you might need an alternate.)

In addition, you'll want to make sure you know where to find a variety of locations in the building. Be sure to ask where the following are:

copy machine	fax machine
mail room	bathrooms
water fountains	refrigerator (to store lunch)
coffee	vending machines
cafeteria	paper and other necessary supplies

I have designed the *Temp Template*® on pages 53 and 54 as a quick reference. It has all the right questions to ask to get the information you need to succeed. Get answers to these questions and you can't fail.

Job upgrade, rate upgrade

If you were sent to do general clerical work at a general clerical rate and the job changes to word-processing secretary, you are entitled to a higher rate of pay. Let the agency know if your job changes drastically, and let the agency handle rate negotiations with their client.

On one of my "secretarial" assignments, within two weeks I had staffed and was running a word-processing center, and had numerous people reporting to me. I told the agency if the company wanted me to handle a "real" job with all the responsibilities that entailed, they would have to pay me "real" money. They did. Don't let companies exploit your knowledge and talent.

Earlier in the chapter, I described the ideal situation, where things were well-planned. A more common scenario is as follows: You are taken to the workstation to find that the vice president you are working for is in a lengthy meeting until lunchtime. You are left alone with an unfamiliar desk, no instructions, and no one knows the password for the computer. This is why you bring personal work. Always carry something to occupy your time: material to read, letters to write, etc.

Initially, when I ended up with nothing to do, I would go from person to person asking if I could assist with any work. I needed overtime money, and I felt compelled to earn it. For the most part I just got startled looks. In some offices, it is a well-kept secret how little

THE TEMP TEMPLATE®
Everything You Need to Know to Survive the First Assignment...and Thereafter

WHO DO I:

...work for?
Get names, telephone numbers and locations for these people. (You'd be surprised how many times this isn't told to you.)

...go to with my questions?
Get name, location and telephone number.

...answer telephones for?
How does the telephone system work? Is there an intercom? How do I answer?

...cover for at lunch?
Who covers for me? Are lunch times "assigned"?

...receive mail for?
Do I distribute it? Open it? Date-stamp it? Where is the date stamp? Where is the mail room? Is mail delivered or do I pick it up?

WHO/WHAT:

...signs my timesheet?
Manager? Personnel? Alternate signer?

...messenger service do I use?
Get telephone and account numbers, and special forms if used.

...car service do I use?
Get telephone and account numbers, and special forms if used.

WHERE IS/ARE THE:

...women's/men's room?
Do I need a key? A code?

...copier?
Are codes or access cards used?

...FAX machine?
Handy list of FAX numbers? Forms or top sheets for the FAX?

...paper and other supplies?

...water fountain, coffee?
Is the coffee free?

...vending machines, cafeteria?
Is the food worth eating? Is it cheap? What are the hours of the cafeteria?

(continued)

THE TEMP TEMPLATE®

(cont.)

1. Ask for a telephone list for people in the department and an internal telephone book.
2. For law firms, get the attorney, client, and matter numbers.
3. Ask for the number to the technical support or LAN administrator.
4. Computer/word processors. Find out the company's document naming protocol and the directory/subdirectory paths for retrieval.
5. When is the last mail pickup? Which courier service does the company use? Where are the forms/envelopes kept? Does service pick up automatically or do I call?

---

work there is and I was upsetting the status quo—speeding up the assembly line, so to speak. Also, it didn't appear that "helping" was acceptable behavior in some corporations. Employees clutched their work with territorial fervor. Work doesn't always happen in a steady flow. There are peaks and valleys; nothing for an hour or two, then you are buried for the next six.

Items to make your life easier

- Always carry an envelope with timesheets from each of your agencies. If, however, you find yourself without the right timesheet on a job, you can use company letterhead (see next page) to write a memo containing the necessary information (your name, the date and time worked, your Social Security number, name and title of your supervisor and your supervisor's signature) in lieu of a timesheet.

- As a temp, you will be subjected to the whims and vagaries of many telephone systems. Some telephone systems emit the wrong tone to pick up messages from your telephone answering machine. This means you must find a pay telephone (never convenient) in order to hear your messages. Consider purchasing a hand-held remote dialer that can be used as a tone recognizer. These items are the size of a pocket calculator and cost around $15 at Radio Shack.

HERITAGE BOX COMPANY
124 Happiness Lane
Meredith, WI 50609

February 27, 1994

Bard Consulting Associates
300 Madison Avenue
New York, NY 10017

This is to confirm that David Jervey worked for us on February 27, 1994, from 9:00 a.m. to 5:00 p.m., less one hour for lunch, for a total of 7 hours. His Social Security number is 565-51-5503.

Henry B. Important (Your Supervisor)
Manager (His/Her Title)

- Cleaner packets for screens and keyboards.
- Alcohol wipes for telephones (you are filling in for sick people).
- Subway and bus maps, and tokens for public transportation.
- Utilize your portable calendar to record the information from your assignment form. Add to it the telephone number you use for the day as well as the person you actually worked for. At the end of the year, your calendar makes a handy permanent record for income tax purposes.
- A paperback dictionary and thesaurus. (I am still amazed at the number of offices that have neither.)

Long-term assignments

An assignment is referred to as "long-term" if it is longer than one or two weeks. Reality is often something entirely different. A long-term assignment can mean anywhere from one day to infinity, especially if it is an "indef," as they say in the trade. The term is usually given to jobs where a permanent person is being sought. Occasionally, it is given to jobs that no one wants for very long. Companies will employ a series of interim workers for these mind-numbing monstrosities, replacing the burned-out temps with fresh horses as needed.

During slow periods, it can be advantageous to take a long-term assignment. In order to earn overtime dollars, you must put in your 40-plus weekly hours at *one* agency. So, if you bounce around on one- and two-day assignments for several agencies, you can easily put in more than 40 hours—but you won't be paid time-and-a-half. The qualifier is that the 40-plus hours must be for one agency, not one company.

Particularly during slow seasons, it's helpful to line up a long-term assignment, if at all possible. Business tends to slow down in weeks with holidays. People leave early, work dwindles. Temps working day-to-day may pick up only two or three days for the week. Try to land a long-term assignment—at least a week-long assignment—over these weeks: President's Day, Memorial Day, Good Friday/Easter, Passover, Fourth of July, Labor Day, Rosh Hashanah, Yom Kippur, Thanksgiving, Christmas and New Year's Eve/Day. You won't be paid for the holidays, but you are assured work on the days preceding and following the holiday.

June is traditionally a sluggish month for professional temps. Try to land a month-long spot. School lets out and all of the eager college students who work for peanuts-an-hour rates hit the agencies. By July, however, the students want to put in some beach time, and the agencies suddenly remember their more seasoned temps.

Another advantage of long-term assignments, for those of you who are looking for a permanent place to park your nameplate, is that companies looking for a long-term person may offer you the job. For that matter, companies *not* looking for a long-term person may offer you the job. Your supervisors may be so impressed with your professionalism, knowledge and productivity, they'll realize they're better off keeping you. (Many times, they are just grateful if temps look corporate, appear to know what they are doing, and don't chew gum. A manager asked me, "What do you *really* do? You seem so *normal*.")

If you take a long-term slot, confirm with your supervisor that the job is continuing at least once a week. A division head may come in one morning and issue an edict, "No more temps." Personnel may announce gleefully that the position has been filled internally and the new person is reporting tomorrow. Either edict can be communicated at 5 p.m. to you, the "disposable" temp, effectively fouling up your schedule for the rest of the week.

When I accept a long-term assignment, the only thing I tell my other agencies is that the job is for a week. First of all, I may not want to stay for two months. If the job works out and I want to do it, I say I've been asked to stay on for another week or two. I take it one week at a time. At any given moment, I maintain relationships with six to eight agencies. During the long-term assignment, I call my counselors every few weeks to touch base, let them know I'm extending for another few weeks, and make sure they have my telephone number. I call between 10 a.m. and 3 p.m. when they aren't as busy.

Staying in touch pays off. If you need work in a hurry because something happened to your assignment, it's nice to have counselors who remember who you are.

Long-term assignment tip

Try to work with the person you are replacing for at least one day prior to her/his leave. It makes for a more orderly transition. This is especially helpful when you are filling in during a maternity leave, or while the company interviews for a permanent replacement. (For administrative/support situations, you shouldn't need more than a day or so of training with the employee.)

Then, ask for a one-day "debriefing" on the job together at the end of the leave. Save filing for the debriefing. Usually the returning person takes right over. Having a pile of filing will give you something to do, and the person who originally set up the filing system will be there to answer questions about where items go. It also serves as a memory jogger for you on what transpired in her/his absence.

On-the-job problems

Here are situations that crop up from time to time. I've tried to provide some solutions that have worked for me.

Everyone tries to give you work. Ask your supervisor to prioritize the work. Tell anyone who proffers work to give it to your supervisor, who will render a decision on its relative importance before passing it along to you. This works every time.

Smoker in area. Ask to sit someplace else, ask for an electric fan, or ask the personnel department for a fan.

Fielding questions about your hourly rate. When other temps ask how much an hour I get, I give them the range that should be paid for the work I am performing. If permanent employees ask, I tell them different work pays different rates, and to check with their personnel department.

Curious employees. Employees sometimes let their curiosity override good manners to ask rude, personal questions. New temps can have mixed feelings and a certain amount of discomfiture about temping. Be as friendly as you choose to be. But you don't owe anyone the story of your life or to the circumstances that led you to temporary work.

Personality conflict. Every now and then, you can run into a situation where the people you are working for don't like you and you know it. Maybe it's because you are self-confident and do the work quickly. Maybe it's because they had attachments to the person who did your job previously. Whatever the reason, they will probably terminate the assignment by the end of the day. Agency and temp professionals are aware of this phenomenon and do not take it to heart. It is not pleasant when it happens, but it's not the end of the world either.

Socializing. In friendly companies, co-workers often include temps in their conversations, office parties and lunch plans. Although nice to be included, it can be a two-edged sword. On the one hand, you want to appear friendly, helpful and pleasant to work with. Yet you want to avoid the perception of spending too much time chatting with co-workers when you have a lot of work to complete. As much as I am touched by the inclusion, it is a burden to me because I have a different agenda. If I'm not doing *their* work, I have my own. Usually, I thank the invitor profusely, then regretfully decline. Temps with different agendas, seeking a permanent job, for instance, may handle this situation differently.

After the novelty wears off

On the first day of an assignment I recommend *always* dressing mainstream corporate, asking for work and agreeing to help whenever asked. After the first day, use discretion. If you become a pest about asking for work, or offering to help (thus upsetting the status quo), you might find yourself out of a job.

Use common sense doing your personal work. Companies have various reactions to people reading at their desks. I've heard a manager say, "We're paying an agency $22 an hour to have her sit there and read a library book? Send her home." I've also had a manager ask me if I had a book to read because there wouldn't be much work for about an hour or so.

Company policies vary. Ask, if you're not sure something is acceptable.

It is always in your best interest to be considered for as many jobs as possible. Counselors don't waste time calling someone who will more than likely refuse the assignment. Try not to place numerous restrictions on the kind of work you accept. To do so reduces your options and the number of offers you will receive, including jobs for which you might be the most qualified. Keep an open mind. Have an adventure or two.

Chapter 4

Managing Multiple Agency Relationships

....

Professional temps are small business owners. They are the sole proprietors of their knowledge and talents, which they lease by the hour. They allow agencies to act as agents in the booking of those hours.

Eight agencies book my services. All of them know that when I temp, I must work five days a week, for the most part, to earn sufficient money. They know also that ours is not an exclusive relationship, except when I'm on one of their assignments. Working for several agencies can be a delicate balancing act at times, but it does establish that your services are in demand.

When I am on the job, the agency I am working for is my only agency, as far as the client knows. If I learn of other job openings in the company, that information goes to the agency placing me on the assignment. To all outward appearances, the agency and I have a perfect relationship.

Bear in mind that the temporary industry is a tight one. Agency personnel know each other, either personally or by reputation, even in large cities. Especially in large cities.

Giving your availability

On the days that you need work, call your agencies between 8 and 8:30 in the morning. Many people find it helps to stand by at an agency. You're there, in plain sight, dressed and ready to go. Especially if you live in the suburbs but work in the city, you have a much better chance of landing an assignment if you're at the agency, rather than if you are home and the agency knows you must commute an hour or so to an assignment.

If you choose to stand by at a central location but are unable to wait at an agency, you might consider waiting in a building with public space, or the "food court" of a local mall. You can do personal work, check messages from public telephones (every 15 minutes when you are looking for an assignment) and receive calls there as well. Meanwhile, the surroundings are pleasant, the bathrooms are fairly clean, and you can sip a coffee forever.

If you're looking for an assignment for the next week, give your availability by Thursday afternoon for the week ahead. Call between 1 and 3:30 p.m., when the agency isn't as busy with incoming orders. As a matter of habit, you should check for messages hourly.

For convenience, keep a list of all the agencies you work for on one page of your planner/organizer with telephone numbers, counselor names (these change), business hours, and timesheet/payday information. This way, no matter where you are, you can refer to it when you need to.

Establish with your agencies how they want to be informed of your availability. When I first started out, I notified all agencies immediately each time I accepted work. Assignments would sometimes be canceled; it is the temporary business. So, I would call everyone *again* to tell them about the cancellation and that I still needed work. I would call them yet again when I got another assignment. I would call them from the job to give my telephone number. I spent a lot of time on the telephone.

Now that I am wiser, I use the following method: Each Thursday afternoon, I inform the agencies I need work. I tell them if I *don't* get an assignment, I will call them again Friday afternoon. If I have work, I call on Monday morning from my assignment with the number where I can be reached.

Let's say I don't pick up an assignment that Thursday. I call the agencies on Friday afternoon to inform them I am still without work. I tell them if I *don't* get an assignment, I will call them at 8 a.m. Monday. If I *do* get work, I will call them after 10 a.m. Monday morning with the telephone number. This method cuts down on the number of telephone calls, and it has worked well for me.

What about schedule conflicts?

What happens if you are offered an assignment for the week and you have a dental appointment on Wednesday afternoon? The dental appointment is *your* scheduling problem, not the agency's. If you get involved in asking the counselor to find out if an absence on Wednesday is acceptable, I can promise you he or she will get someone else for the job. Agencies don't want a hassle, and they don't want to risk annoying the client.

Accept the assignment. Chances are you'll be able to work something out—either by coming in early, working through lunch, or staying late. The worst that can happen is you'll reschedule your appointment. (As a rule, I'd advise scheduling all personal appointments for Wednesdays, Thursdays and Fridays. Give yourself a couple of days to settle into an assignment before having to manipulate hours or ask for time off.)

How choosy should you be?

In my first eight months as a temp, I had to "stand by" six times—meaning that I hadn't found work for the week, or something happened with the assignment (it was canceled, I wasn't needed for a full week, etc.). I was without work only three of those days. I used the time to sign up at other agencies and to handle some personal matters I hadn't found time for.

As I've said before, keep an open mind about the assignments you are offered. (This is still hard for me to do.) As you gain experience you will find some assignments that sound great will be grim, and vice versa. Say yes whenever possible. You only have to commit mentally for one day at a time.

In terms of jobs, I have my own list of preferences. I don't want a long commute since time is money. I don't like dictaphones, busy telephones and, because of allergies, I can't have smokers nearby. Yet I have to compromise at times in order to work steadily, especially during slow periods.

The Recession has brought a reduction in the number of one-day jobs. Companies seem to "make do" for a day or two. The adjustments I have made are to take more long-term work of one, two or three months than I would under different circumstances. I am less choosy about location and will commute for longer distances. Before the Recession hit, I was able to secure week-long assignments (my preference) consistently.

Marketing your services to agencies

Don't be afraid to engage in a little self-promotion. Let your counselor know of any compliments you receive, and especially if clients say they will ask for you again. It doesn't hurt to leave your name and agency telephone number on a rolodex card with the client. Write down your special skills—for example, "Temp Lotus Expert," or "Temp Accountant."

By the same token, record the name of the complimenting person, and his or her comment, in your organizer. You might interview for a permanent job within the company in the future, and that information may be helpful.

From time to time, you may go through a period where one or more of your agencies seldom has work for you. Don't hesitate to sign up at a new agency if that happens. It's an ego-booster to have an agency excited that you are joining them and eager to put you to work.

Agency personnel changes frequently. Make an effort to introduce yourself to the new counselor, in person, if convenient. Occasionally, you may end up working with someone you don't get along with. When that happens, concentrate on obtaining assignments from your other agencies, or sign up at new ones. Don't end all contact with the problem agency. The counselor may be passing through on the way to yet another "opportunity."

Even if an agency has infrequent assignments, keep in touch periodically. The only constant in temporary employment is change. They might come up with a terrific job when you need it most.

Assignment problems: Who handles what?

Part of the typical agency spiel is to instruct you to call if there are any problems on the job, "any problems at all."

All jobs have annoyances; most of them you can work out for yourself. Use the agencies only for serious situations you can't resolve satisfactorily. Call them for run-of-the-mill matters and they'll think you're a pain to work with.

For example, here is how I handle a problem that crops up from time to time. I am allergic to tobacco smoke. Once or twice a year I end up next to a smoker. The first thing I do is ask for an electric fan. If there isn't one in the area, I ask to borrow one from another area. If that isn't possible, I ask my supervisor if I might sit elsewhere. I have called my contact in personnel (whom I met when she took me to the work station) and asked to borrow a fan.

If all of those attempts fail, I call the agency and ask to be replaced. I do not ask the smoker to stop smoking. I feel to do so will only add more unpleasantness to an already unpleasant situation. Only once in six years have I asked to be replaced because I couldn't resolve the smoke situation myself.

Following are examples of problems you may encounter:

Asking to be replaced. Use this option judiciously and sparingly. If the assignment is a horror and you cannot tactfully correct the situation, call the agency. Tell your counselor that you will finish the day but do not wish to continue, and explain why. Don't walk off the job and *then* call—unless, of course, you are in some kind of danger. Then run first and call later.

Client wants private deal. Whether you say yes or no, this is *always* a sticky situation. On the timesheet, the client is asked to sign a statement that says to the effect:

> *We understand that this person is an employee of Abstruse Temporary Service. In the event we employ this person on our payroll (or in a consulting capacity) within 90 days after completion of the assignment, we agree to pay Abstruse Temporary Service a fee.*

I don't take the high moral ground on this issue. There are very practical reasons I don't cut deals. I have good working relationships with my agencies, and I intend to keep it that way. I have neither the desire nor the time to establish and maintain a freelance practice; I use the agencies as bookers. For their 40 percent to 50 percent mark-up, the agencies find clients, service the accounts and sometimes wait three or four months for payment. Working through agencies, I know I will receive a weekly check that won't bounce.

In addition, I tell the agency when I have been approached so they can exercise some caution in whom they send to the company in the future.

No matter how tactfully you handle this situation, clients who try to cut out the agency fee will not have you back because they want someone who will deal. This means they will possibly tell the agency your work is unsatisfactory. Another reason to let the agency know you were approached.

If you succumb to temptation and accept the client's proposition, you leave yourself vulnerable to hassles, games with paychecks and the agency finding out. Who wants the problems attached to seeking redress if the client decides to pay you considerably less than the rate you agreed on?...Or not at all?

Two assignment offers. An agency may call to line up your services while you're still awaiting the confirmation of an assignment. You may commit, awaiting final confirmation. If you do this and another offer comes in, tell the counselor you are waiting to hear about a job. If he or she can wait five minutes, and the earlier offer isn't firm, you will accept the assignment. Call the first counselor and verify yes or no, then proceed accordingly. An unconfirmed job offer does not always come to fruition.

A better offer. What if you are offered a higher hourly rate for an assignment with a different agency after you have accepted another offer? By all means accept the better offer and cancel the earlier assignment—if you want to destroy your reputation and end your relationship with the first agency.

When I have accepted a one-day spot and a week-long offer occurs, I may go to the first agency and ask if they will release me, provided, of course, they can replace me. Before I do anything, I tell the second agency I will try to get released from a prior assignment. If, however, the agency is unable to find a substitute, or says no for a legitimate reason, I honor the first commitment.

The two-way street. As you know, a company may book your services for a month, then cancel the order before you arrive, or change its mind after a few days and decide not to fill the position—or not to fill it with you at any rate. A company can do this; it is, after all, the temporary business.

You accepted a two-month assignment in good faith. Two weeks into it, a consulting project you have been pitching to one of your clients has come to fruition and needs your immediate attention. Or, perhaps, by the end of the first week, the assignment itself has deteriorated into a daily ordeal. Call the agency. Tell your counselor you must leave the assignment and why, and offer to remain for a day or two while he or she lines up your replacement. This is, after all, the temporary business.

Circumstances can change. Temps are not indentured servants forced to endure a term of service. Don't subscribe to a double standard.

Favorite counselor leaves agency. The industry has a high turnover rate. When counselors go on to new opportunities, usually the temp is among the last to know. A common ploy is to have another counselor take the calls, saying so-and-so is busy, out of the office, whatever. Industry protocol prohibits the departed counselors from making contact with their former temps. Co-workers succumb to group amnesia as to the whereabouts of their former colleague.

Sometimes the job-changer's new agency advertises her/his arrival in the Sunday classifieds. Unless you like reading classified ads, you will miss the announcement. How do you find the counselor? Asking other temps sometimes works.

I tell my favorites how much I enjoy working with them. I mention the high industry turnover, ask that they keep in touch when they go on to other jobs, and give them a self-addressed, stamped postcard...discreetly.

Offered low hourly rate. Over the past six years, I have developed a relationship of mutual trust with several agencies. When things are slow, I encourage counselors to offer jobs even if they are not at my regular rate. There might be other factors to consider in the decision; in my case, blocks of time to write. I give counselors a range to work within.

Suppose you are offered a rate much lower than your normal one. Suppose your usual rate is $18 but the counselor says, "I can pay $16 an hour for this spot." You can counteroffer with, "Why don't we meet halfway? Can you pay $17?"

Agencies are well aware that a low rate doesn't always buy value. Their reputation and continued business with the client depends on how often they send a person who performs well on the job. Sometimes that means taking a smaller percentage of the fee.

Ask if you can meet halfway. Usually there is room to negotiate. When agreement can't be reached and I feel I can't accept the assignment at the rate they're offering, I still thank them for thinking of me and ask to be kept in mind for other jobs.

Timesheets/paycheck. Your assignment is not convenient to the agency. It is time-consuming and out of your way to deliver timesheets and pick up paychecks. The mail is not especially reliable.

Most agencies will work with you to rectify the situation, giving approval to call in hours or fax the timesheet, turning in the signed timesheet when you pick up the paycheck. I have had agencies willing to cut a check on called-in hours, mail my check a day early, and accept my timesheet (mailed on Friday after work) whenever it arrived.

You want more money. The job requires more skill than was requested and should command a higher rate. For example, a company describes a clerical position, then assigns complex projects that require computer knowledge. I suggest informing the agency of the circumstances and asking for more money. Don't *be* exploited, don't *feel* exploited. Libraries have many good books on negotiation if this isn't one of your strong suits.

Time off or illness during a long-term assignment. Of course, when you're mostly scheduling short-term assignments, you can take time off simply by not requesting an assignment for a particular day or week. But when you're on a long-term assignment, the rules are a little nebulous. After all, you're not a full-time employee, entitled to two weeks' vacation and five sick days per year. Yet there you are, on a three-month job, and you become ill, or you need a few days off for personal reasons.

I arrange it with the client if I need time off. Whenever possible I try to have my absence:

- Not conflict with a heavy workload.
- Coincide with the supervisor's out-of-town or vacation absence.
- Covered by another temp if someone is needed to work in my place.

After the arrangements are made, I inform my counselor. Agency personnel count on a certain amount of income based on the number of employed temps, and my not working affects this.

In the case of illness, I notify the client first, then call the agency.

Notify agency

Throughout the book, I stress how *you*, the temp, are in charge of what happens on the job and managing the relationships with agencies. However, certain types of information or changes should be relayed to the agency as soon as possible. Here are some:

1. **The assignment has been extended, or it has ended sooner than expected.** One-day assignments can turn into a two- or three-month project leading to a permanent job offer. Your week-long assignment can terminate because of lack of work, company politics, or changing needs. The agency needs this information.

2. **You are offered a full-time position.** Under the contract with the client, the agency is entitled to a fee if you accept a full-time position. They may choose to waive it or reduce it in order to keep the client happy—but that's their decision, and they must be informed if this situation comes up.

3. **Upgraded responsibilities.** Your job as "queen of the copy machine" has transformed into "financial analyst of the hour" because the manager learned of your background. This entitles you to more money. Let the agency negotiate the rate.

4. **Illness or an emergency renders you unable to report to (or stay on) job as planned.** The agency will need to get a one-day fill-in, or to replace you if needed.

5. **Your skill base has increased.** You have worked on Lotus 1-2-3 all week and can now take assignments requiring "light" Lotus skills, which means more money. Let your counselor know about your new knowledge as soon as possible.

6. **Change in your availability for work.** Keep your availability status current. It saves useless telephone calls for all concerned.

7. **Client approaches you about working without agency.** Some clients will tell the agency that you are not doing a good job for them if you refuse to work privately. Protect yourself.

8. **On-the-job problem you are unable to resolve.** You are expected to work in a semi-construction zone, complete with copious amounts of flying dust and the noise of power tools. No one is willing to find you a better work environment. Call the agency.

    This actually happened to me. The agency was unable to resolve the problem. I left mid-day.

9. **You are injured on job.** A faulty file drawer pulls all the way out and drops onto your foot, injuring it. Notify the agency. Your hands are covered with paper cuts from working on files. Painful, yes. Call the agency? No.

As the business climate improves, lean corporations have the option to rehire staff or to turn to consultants and temporary professionals. At this time, it appears that a large number of them are choosing to go with contingency workers. Perhaps this will change as the economy grows more stable and corporations become less nervous. However, while it is occurring, there is a wealth of opportunity out there for temps who manage their time, skill and experience as small businesses. Juggling relationships with numerous agencies is no more difficult than managing any group of business relationships. Temps who do it well will have the competitive edge.

Resources

The Haggler's Handbook: One Hour to Negotiating Power, Leonard Koren and Peter Goodman, W.W. Norton & Company, 1991.

Getting What You Want, Kare Anderson, Dutton, 1993.

Bargaining Games, John Keith Murnigham, Morrow, 1992.

Getting Past No, William Ury, Bantam, 1993.

Getting to Yes, Roger Fisher, Houghton Mifflin, 1991.

Chapter 5

Maximizing
On-The-Job Efficiency

••

Professional temps often remind me of world travelers. As they go from company to company, they become sophisticated about other "cultures" and methods of approaching a project. The ones who run their temping as small businesses, often in conjunction with another vocation, are ingenious in organizing assignments to dispatch work expeditiously. This chapter is devoted to passing along their tips.

As discussed in an earlier chapter, one of the advantages of temping is that often, while you're on assignment, you will have blocks of free time in which you can work on personal projects. And the more organized and efficient you are, the more work you can do for the client and for yourself. Yet whether you're balancing your checkbook, learning a new software program or writing a novel, *without exception, the client's work is completed first!*

Your goal is to work as efficiently as possible. You want to do an excellent job as a professional temp as well as meet your personal goals. In order to do that, you must be organized.

General preparation from home

First, organize for a weekly agenda as well as a daily one. Then, devise a follow-up system that works for you. We discussed in Chapter 1 the value of a good organizer/planner. I use a combination of the monthly, yearly and weekly calendars of my organizer and my wall year-at-a-glance calendar to keep track of my schedule and deadlines. It may not be the best system, but it works for me.

Popular follow-up tools you might want to investigate are the "tickler" systems, or desk files/sorters that open like a book. Most of the systems have 31 partitions for the days of the month, indexed in some fashion. The desk files usually have months-of-the-year tabs as well.

Late Sunday afternoon I plan and organize work for the week. This can take up to one hour if I have big plans for the week. I make a three-column to-do list of everything I need to accomplish. The columns are entitled: "Must Do," "Should Do," and "Can Do." Then, I pull out files, letters, research material, telephone numbers—whatever I need for the entire week. I separate them into categories and place them in the appropriate colored, labeled folder. I select several items to pack with my temp stuff for the next morning. I also pack my lunch ahead of time. The less thinking I have to do in the morning, the better. Each weekday morning, I select a few more items to complete on the job.

You should start each day with a plan for what you want to accomplish, and a to-do list. Use expandable, letter-size plastic file envelopes to transport your personal work back and forth from job to home. These envelopes come in several colors, are lightweight and won't get dog-eared. Use a colored "completed" folder inside the file envelope to carry home completed work. It saves time packing and unpacking, or looking through folders.

After I arrive home, before I get too relaxed, I unpack for the day. Using my list prepared on the job, I repack for the next day. That way I don't have to think in the morning.

On the job: Starting out right

Start off every temp assignment—by preparing for your departure. All pros leave behind a brief written report about the work they completed on an assignment. Some write personal notes, others leave a list or fill out a form they have designed and photocopied. The "completed work" form on the next page will give you some ideas.

Label a manila folder "completed work." As you finish projects during the course of your assignment, place copies of completed work inside the folder. Attach a note explaining what you did, where you put things, how you have named documents, and any other pertinent information that would be helpful.

If you don't like to write notes, design a form such as the one on the next page that can be completed and left behind to simplify the process of imparting information.

Finding your way around

Just figuring out the lay of the land can often be the most difficult challenge in tackling a temp assignment. Imagine that your spacecraft has landed on another planet. You do not know where anything is, you do not know the population's strange ways. The alien-manager greets you, speaking the jargon-language of his or her particular corporation, and gives you instructions on how to do the work, forgetting that you are not "one of them." Depending upon your responsibilities, the size of the company, the number of people or departments you must interact with and other factors, it could take days before you figure out the who, what and where of it all.

You are not without resources. First, there are the "right" questions to ask from your *Temp Template*®, shown on pages 53 and 54. Here, too, are additional things you can do to bring order to the chaos.

Simplify the departmental telephone list. Make a photocopy of it and highlight the frequently called names. If no list exists, and the department size is a manageable number, compile one and leave it behind when you go.

Make an office "seating chart." It doesn't take much time to hand-write an office seating chart for your general area to help you find people quickly.

Compose a quick-reference internal distribution list that includes locations and telephone numbers. Every time you send material inter-department, add the pertinent information to your list.

Completed Work

Documents

For	Document name/Location	Description
1. Sarah Smith	c:\wp51\docs\ss-1-20.mem	memo to R. Anderson
2.		
3.		
4.		
5.		

Travel Arrangements

For	Date of Trip	Arrangement
1.		
2.		
3.		
4.		
5.		

Meetings Scheduled

For	Date	Meet Who	Where
1.			
2.			
3.			
4.			
5.			

Telephone Messages

For	Caller	Date/Time	Telephone #
1.			
2.			
3.			
4.			
5.			

Temp's Name: _____ Agency:_____

Date: _____

Replace plain message pads, if you can, with ones that make carbonless copies of calls. This gives you an archive of calls received during your tenure and a reference tool to find people quickly.

Make up a pile of buck slips or labels for internal distribution. On most assignments, you will find that you circulate materials to the same few people.

Change the phone mail greeting to reflect your presence if you will be there for a week or longer.

> *"Clara Smith's line. This is Diane Thrailkill. I'm filling in for Clara while she attends a sales meeting this week. Please leave a message, including your name and telephone number."*

Change back to the standard greeting at the end of the assignment. Let the employee know that her greeting needs to be personalized again.

Now, to get yourself organized

For assignments of at least one week, it pays to take the time to organize the workstation. You have the advantage of coming into a position with an open mind and a fresh pair of eyes. Look at the job as though you were a consultant; make it better for yourself.

Sometimes it takes no more than rearranging the desk, or making simple changes like moving materials you use frequently to the front of the file drawer. Unfamiliar work that can be found easily and dispatched quickly gives you more free time. At the end of the assignment, replace everything as you found it.

First, organize the desk file drawer for your convenience. I don't mean you should redo the system that the permanent employee has set up. But you should pull forward the files that you'll be using frequently during your assignment, and create a few of your own: such as frequently needed information including phone numbers, organization charts, etc.

Also, on longer assignments, and ones in which you will clearly be able to work on some of your own projects, set up your personal files.

Over time you will probably develop your own system of organization. Whatever you devise, I suggest setting up handy personal files in your desk drawer. I use colored hanging files and folders. That way, I can find what I need with a glance.

- Red: "Telephone calls." The folder holds background material needed for various matters that take a call.
- Green: "Enter data." Information to be entered onto lists, updates for mailings, etc. Work I can do on automatic pilot.
- Blue: "Compose." Letters to write, publicity blurbs.
- Orange: "Resources." Helpful directories or reference material.

If you spend a lot of time looking for things, at home or on the job, or you can't seem to get to the projects you want to, even though you have chunks of free time at work, you need to organize yourself better. There are many books about organizing and time management, which could help you. In addition, consider these "peak productivity" tips, as well:

- Group tasks for maximum efficiency on the job. For instance, do a block of telephone calls, or compose several short letters.
- Try to finish one task before starting another.
- Before leaving the assignment at the end of the afternoon, make a list of materials you need to bring from home for the next day: correspondence, telephone numbers, reference materials.
- Determine the time of day you are most productive. Some people keep a detailed task log, recording activities every half-hour to do this.
- Schedule important work for productive hours; do the mindless tasks (stuffing envelopes, verifying information by telephone) during your least productive times.

Leave the campsite a better place

What are the ways temps distinguish themselves so that companies ask for them by name? By taking the old Girl Scout motto to heart and leaving a nonthreatening improvement behind to make the worksite a better place. In addition to leaving completed work in a folder with a note attached, here are some ideas to get you started.

1. Print out directories for diskettes, place in the jackets or tape to the front of jackets. (Educating those who place indecipherable scribbles on the label that there just might be a better way to do it.)
2. Set up templates for memos or for using envelopes in the printer. Leave simple written instructions.
3. "Computerize" a form the employees use a typewriter to complete. For instance, medical forms: Certain information—name, address, birth date, Social Security number—must be completed with every claim. Once the form is on a computer, that information never has to be filled in again.

   At one company I placed the medical form in a shared library on their network. I left instructions for its use with my personnel contact and asked her to relay the information to all of the secretaries after I left.
4. Leave a one-page instruction sheet explaining the position to a "temporary employee." I do this when I'm in the spot for longer than a week. Think how much more a company would get for its "temp dollar" with something like the example on the next page.

General problem-solving

In his helpful and unusual book, *Thriving in Tough Times* (Career Press), Paul G. Fox has a "Creativity Checklist" that lists nine ways to look at solving a problem; ways, perhaps, that you might not have thought of before. I feel his method has useful applications for many areas of life, not just portraying super temp on the job.

1. Can the object or process be put to *other uses*? New ways to use? Other uses if modified?
2. Can the object or process be *adapted*? What else is like this? What other ideas does this suggest? Does the past offer a parallel? What could I copy? Whom could I emulate?
3. Can the object or process be *modified*? New twist? Change meaning, color, motion, sound, odor, form, shape, use?

Instructions for the temporary secretary
(example)

General: The "Daily Appointment Forms" are in red folder on desk. Ron must fill one out and give to Reggie (mail person) by 10 a.m.

                     Make two copies of all memos and letters. Please leave in blue folder marked "File."

Messengers: Notify Frances in Reception (0) and she will call the messenger. Prepare the package or envelope and take to her for pick up.

Supplies: Stationery is in the first drawer under the PC. Envelopes and junk paper are under the printer. The hall supply closet has other office supplies.

Telephones: Your extension is 229, Ron Smith is 231, Sarah Allen is 241. Please answer "Communications." Both Ron and Sarah will pick up calls if they are in the office. Please answer for them on the third ring.

                     Press 9 for an outside line. For area codes outside 212, press 81, wait for a tone, then press area code and number. Reception can be reached by pressing 0. A list of telephone numbers for other staff members is taped to the top pullout section on right-hand side of desk.

PC: When you turn on the PC you will go into Norton Commander. Press F2 for the selection menu to access Multimate. Select MULTIMATE and press ENTER.

Printer: If printer stops and the letters FE light up, that means the ribbon needs to be reversed or changed. PO means there is no paper.

4. Can the object or process be *magnified*? What to add? More time? Greater frequency? Stronger? Higher? Longer? Thicker? Extra value? Duplicate? Multiply?

5. Can the object or process be *minimized*? Made smaller? Condensed? Miniaturized? Lower? Shorter? What to subtract or leave out? Streamline? Split up?

6. Can the object or process be *substituted*? What else? Who else? Other ingredient? Other material? Other process? Other place? Other approach? Other tone of voice?

7. Can the object or process be *rearranged*? Interchange parts? Other pattern? Other layout? Other sequence? Change pace? Change schedule?

8. Can the object or process be *reversed*? Turn it backward? Turn it upside down? Reverse it? Reverse roles? Turn tables? Turn the other cheek?

9. Can the object or process be *combined*? How about a blend? An alloy? An assortment? Combine units? Combine purposes? Combine appeals? Combine ideas?

Just a few precautions

Use great care and tact when presenting suggestions for improvement. People are territorial and can be defensive about their way of doing things. Certainly don't argue the point with them.

Be sure that any materials or books that you bring into the company are clearly marked with your name to avoid any unpleasant confusion about ownership.

More tips—to increase the size of your paycheck

Here are six relatively painless ways to enlarge your weekly temping paycheck. The first four can be done immediately; the remaining two will pay over time.

1. Hourly pay is calculated in quarter-hour increments. Limit your lunch break to 15 minutes. Or bring your lunch and eat at your desk while you work. You are there to earn money, not to enrich your soul.

2. Bring a lunch whenever possible. Don't waste time looking for a reasonable place to eat.

3. Schedule personal errands before and after work, rather than during a lunch break.

4. Each morning arrive 15 minutes to a half-hour early and get right to work. You will be surprised how quickly the extra time adds up to a fatter paycheck. Most of the time your supervisor will be pleased at your initiative and eagerness to work. Use common sense here. Do this only if there is enough work to warrant it.

   Note: Managers who do not want you to put in extra hours will make it a point to tell you. I leave my timesheet on the desk so it can be looked over at any time. When there is a surfeit of work, rare is the manager who doesn't want you to do it.

5. Become computer literate, no matter what your specialty is. Apprentice yourself to someone by offering to do mundane tasks for a little instruction. Use free time to learn more.

6. Take every opportunity to learn another software package on the job, and be paid for learning. Be a volunteer.

   Suppose someone asks if you know Lotus 1-2-3. You can answer that you have "played around" with it a little, or you can immediately find out if a complicated procedure is wanted. Most of the time, you will be asked to do glorified data entry, but it gets you using a new software package. Someone will give you some brief instructions to get you started. Get a copy of the manual. Teach yourself more functions. After you have worked in the new software, let your agencies know about it but don't inflate your proficiency. More skill, more money.

Off-the-job tip: Computer skills equal more money

Learning how to use the computer takes a commitment of time and energy that is more akin to learning a musical instrument than learning how to program your VCR. It will, however, pay off in a higher temp rate, or a better salary if your goal is a permanent job. Inexpensive classes can usually be found through local adult and continuing education programs for nearby school districts, colleges and community centers.

Consider calling instructors to ask about private sessions. Two or so hours of concentrated instruction will rarely cost more than a class and would be a better use of your time. Here are a few more suggestions:

1. Take the time to learn one software program really well. After that, the world is yours. Each software package in a genre (such as word processing, spreadsheet, database) will use the same logic and similar, if not the same, functions. The difference will be the key strokes used for the execution. But, you need to be familiar with the full range of genre functions in order to learn the next program easily.

2. Don't sign up for instruction until you are able to use the program afterwards. The old adage, "use it or lose it" applies to computers, too.

3. Don't try to learn two programs simultaneously—you will confuse them. I meet far too many job seekers who have signed up for WordPerfect and Lotus classes. I try to talk them into dropping one program until they are more comfortable with the computer in general, have learned and are *using* a program.

4. If you don't have a home computer, you might want to look into renting a workstation at an hourly rate through a "public computer" rental service in your area. If you can't find listings for them in the telephone classified pages, try asking computer stores for referrals.

Landing on a strange planet isn't easy. But once you have worked at a few temp assignments, you will develop your own routine and a sense of what needs to be done—and you'll be surprised at how quickly and successfully you'll adapt to an alien culture.

For those of you taking assignments using the computer, be sure to take a look at the next chapter for even more time-saving and organizing tips.

Chapter 6

All Things Computer

··

As a temp and a consultant, I continually see people using computers as expensive typewriters, reentering the same information over and over again. The biggest favor you can do for yourself is to learn functions that enable you to use technology strategically, to automate repetitive tasks and to perform routine work effortlessly. While the tips here are for the IBM/DOS environment, Windows and Macintosh users should read them to familiarize themselves with the kinds of problems that can crop up on assignment, then adapt solutions to their environments.

To the axiom, "Time is money," add "Enter information once."

Finding your way around a strange computer

There are a number of useful software tools that can be of great help to you. However, just as you do with the new work environment, you must first find your way around your new computer. Two software packages that I find are helpful for this are Magellan and Word for Word. Both are user-friendly and need a minimum amount of time and effort to learn.

Magellan, a utility package, has a scanning function that allows me to find unfamiliar documents quickly without going into the file itself, a real boon when working with new material.

Word for Word is a conversion software that lets me take documents into a more flexible software package. For instance, companies in the middle of changing over to a different word processing package might have a portion of their current documents in an old version of WordStar. It makes more sense to convert the documents to new software, rather than work in an inflexible and cumbersome package.

If you aren't familiar with these software packages, it might be worthwhile to visit your local software store and have demonstrations of these and similar packages. *PC Magazine* and *PC Computing* magazines are good sources to find information and performance reviews on available IBM-environment software. *MacGuide* and *MacUser* magazines do the same thing for the Macintosh environment.

Here are some more tips:

Carry a simple utility program with you daily. Utility programs provide fast, easy ways to copy, find, move, erase, view and manage files. Office personnel are often vague as to the location of their document files, and very few have a naming protocol, much less one that makes sense. A utility program gives you the ability to find unfamiliar files easily, as well as to perform routine maintenance functions. Some programs you might consider are:

- **IBM:**   Norton, Xtree, Magellan, PC Tools, Q-DOS
- **Macintosh:**   DiskTools Plus, DiskTop

Generally, you can find any document with one of these tools; all are good and relatively inexpensive.

Print out the directories for the diskettes you are to use. Tape the directory to the diskette jacket. It takes the guesswork out of what files are on them. If you're new to computers, here's how to do it:

At the A:\ or B:\ prompt, type: *DIR* (press ENTER) to list the files. Press *Print Screen*, to print the list.

Carry blank diskettes with you daily. When you need one, you usually need it *now*. (Your printer stops working, someone else must use your computer for awhile.) Diskettes can be hard to come by in some places. Rather than spend an hour trying to get one, I carry my own formatted, low-density, brightly colored diskettes for easy identification—one 3 1/2" and one 5 1/4" sizes. (Remember: Low-density diskettes will work on high-density drives, but the reverse is not true. High-density diskettes do not work on low-density drives.)

Set up templates in several word processing packages for envelopes, faxes, memos, labels, courier forms. Keep these together on a separate diskette. I have templates in Microsoft Word, WordPerfect and MultiMate, on 3 1/2" and 5 1/4" diskettes. All I have to do is copy the file, make any adjustments (different make of printer, for instance), and I'm in business.

Automate routine functions (typing repetitive phrases, invoking editing functions such as boldface, italics, subscript, etc.) using macros. Macros are a set of instructions that are executed by one or two keystrokes. An example of a repetitive short phrase would be the closing of a letter. Instead of typing the same closing, name and title for endless letters (your own correspondence included), you would press one or two keys to activate the macro; the phrase types itself.

If you are unfamiliar with macros, get the software manual and teach yourself how to do them. It is not a difficult operation; learning how to use it will save you time and energy. As you did with templates, save the macros on diskettes and edit them as needed on the job. Don't reinvent the wheel for each assignment.

Place footers that tell the file name and path on all work. Some temps use the automatic date code in footers to accurately track updates.

Use mail merges to quickly dispatch multiple letters. Teach yourself how to do it if you don't already know.

Set up an archive for old documents. People use hard disks as vast storage bins, naming each and every fragment of data. This results in temps searching for files in a morass of unfamiliar names. Create a new subdirectory called "current." Use it for work that you do during the assignment. This will go a long way toward speeding up searches for files.

At the end of the assignment you can copy the "current" documents back into the general or copy the "current" directory onto a diskette and delete it from the hard disk. Or you can leave instructions for the permanent employee how to get into the subdirectory. Let her/him make the decision of what to do with it. Assume a lack of knowledge on the part of the employee and write explicit directions.

Use a variety of colored paper for different drafts of documents that undergo numerous revisions. It prevents the mix-ups that often occur with several versions floating around.

Carry software/equipment help-line numbers with you. What happens when you have questions—and *no one* knows what to do? Call equipment and software help lines, which should be posted on the equipment, in the owner's manuals or printed materials that come with the software. To get help from the technical support staff, you must have available the serial number of the equipment or software, the company name and your name. Start compiling a list of numbers for the equipment and software you work with. If you don't find help numbers readily, call the company's main number and ask.

Save documents frequently, especially if you are part of a LAN (local area network). Having several hours of work wiped out because of electrical fluctuations or network failures is more than depressing.

Protect yourself from computer viruses. As a precaution, your home computer should have virus protection software if you are going to do personal work on the job, which is later copied onto your hard disk.

Get paid to go to school

Carry with you software you are in the process of learning and exploring to use on the "A" drive. For instance, you can teach yourself how to use a virus program or to "unerase" deleted files when there is no emergency. The best way to figure out what to do in a crisis is to *not* be in the middle of one while you're learning.

When workstations have a manual for the software you have been hired to use, learn another function or two, or some shortcuts.

On my first temporary assignment, my "Do you have any work I can do?" requests produced startled looks, not work. So I took the MultiMate manual and literally went from A to Z, teaching myself unfamiliar functions. Then I compiled a shortcut sheet, which I shared with the other secretaries (to more startled looks) and, later, with other temps.

Advanced word-processing/computer tips

For those of you who are more experienced with computers, here are tips that will speed up the organization of an assignment (or a department). Managers, in particular, will find ideas to pass along to administrative and support staffs.

Institute a naming protocol for any documents you create to convey as much information about the document or file as possible. To get you started, here are a few helpful extensions to use with packages that accept custom extensions:

General:	report	docname.RPT
	template	docname.TEM
	list	docname.LST
	memo	docname.MEM
	letter	docname.LTR
	chart	docname.CHT
	labels	docname.LAB
Legal:	brief	docname.BRF
	matter	docname.MAT
	contract	docname.CON

Build a correspondence name and address list using "external copy" or the "cut-and-paste" functions. This enables you to quickly find and print out unfamiliar addresses on envelopes or labels. Here is a simple way to do this, using "cut and paste."

1. Save the file after typing the letter.
2. Highlight and copy the name and address to the buffer ("cut").
3. Close the letter file.
4. Create a new file "cor.lst" (correspondence list).
5. Recall the name and address from the buffer ("paste" copied address). Save the file.

Each time you type a letter, add the name and address alphabetically to "cor.lst" where it can be easily found later to "cut and past" on a label or envelope.

Do all word-processing correspondence on separate pages of one document, unless specifically told to do otherwise. This keeps the client's work organized and in one place for easy access. I make the first page a log where I record who wrote the letter or memo, who received it, the date and the subject. The second page is the most current document. The last page of the file is the first document of the week (or month). I print out the log and leave it for the regular secretary. The log has the file name as a footer. (See the example on the next page.)

On longer assignments, set up monthly correspondence files for documents. Thus, May-94.COR, JUNE-94.COR holds correspondence for the months of May and June, 1994.

Devise a system to prevent accidental deletion or overwriting of data. Several people working on the same project should come up with a method that all understand and agree to *before* beginning the project. Transporting personal files on two sizes of floppies to work at home and on the assignment also requires a system.

Document Log for Week of 12/10/91
(example)

(The log itself is page 1)

12/14	(page 2)	MJB letter to Harold Smith re resignation
12/13	(page 3)	ARB memo to Drafting Department re specs
12/12	(page 4)	ARB letter to Human Resources re vacation
12/10	(page 5)	ARB letter to Martha Covey re fees

(Document name and path appears as a footer.
Document name "translation" is: Correspondence for
week of Dec. 10.)
c:\mm\docs\wk12-10.cor

For instance, I use a simple method for personal work that utilizes a date and designated location as part of the file name. Thus, a file called "chap1-6.04c" was edited last on June 4 and saved on the hard disk at the job. The designated locations are:

A: 5 1/4" diskettes (The file name will incorporate A.)

B: 3 1/2" diskettes (The file name will incorporate B.)

C: Assignment on hard disk (Work saved on the hard disk of client computer will incorporate C.)

D: Home hard disk (Work saved on home hard disk will incorporate D.)

After "chap1-6.04c" is edited the next day, it is copied from the hard disk to the 3 1/2" diskette to be transferred home.

The letter will change to "b" and the date will change to June 5 (chap1-6.05b). When it is copied onto the hard drive at home, the letter will change to "d" (chap1-6.05d).

Troubleshooting on the job

Believe it or not, what follows is *not* a rare scenario: The computer you are to use is protected by a menu needing a password. The person you are filling in for left no written instructions that include a password. No one in the department or in technical support knows it either. What do you do? While you are waiting for a supervisor to solve the problem, there are a few quick and dirty things that often work in IBM environments. Let me emphasize that these suggestions are to get you through a simple menu deterrent, and in no way should be construed as misguided instruction on how to become a hacker.

A. Bypass the Menu and enter the software program from its subdirectory.

1. Escape from the Menu program. Usually the ESC key or a Function key will do it. The menu itself might instruct users with a "Return to DOS" or a "Leave Menu Program" and the function key or command to execute it.

2. Do a DIR command to find out the subdirectory of the software you wish to use. Change to that subdirectory. Do another DIR if you are unsure of the command to activate the software. Execution commands have the extension .EXE or .COM. Execute the appropriate command to activate the software.

B. Use the A drive to enter the subdirectory on C:\. Another approach you can use is to boot from A: with your copy of DOS. Then change the drive to C: and follow step 2 above.

C. Determine the password form the autoexec file. Type the command TYPE AUTOEXEC.BAT (press ENTER). The commands in the autoexec.bat file will be displayed on the screen. The password should be in the last word or two.

D. Break the code. Many people use some combination of their first names, initials or nicknames as passwords. Once I used a pet's name from its snapshot tacked to the bulletin board—and it worked. Try a few combinations. This is successful maybe 25 percent of the time.

Just a few precautions

Be cautious about displaying extensive knowledge of computers. People illiterate in matters technical sometimes get nervously suspicious that you are spreading computer viruses or stealing their company's secrets.

As with any other material you bring with you, be sure that personal diskettes are clearly marked with your name. Consider using the brightly colored ones. Rare is the company that buys hot pink or safety yellow diskettes for its employees.

Keep personal on-the-job computer work in a private subdirectory or on diskette.

To your good health: Computer-related injuries

Over time, those who use computers can develop injuries with painful symptoms. This is an insidious problem; typing on a computer keyboard seems so benign. To give you some idea of why injury occurs, consider that typing 60 words per minute for six hours executes 100,000 strokes, the equivalent of at least 1,500 pounds of total force through the thumbs and fingertips.

The two most common forms of injury are carpal tunnel syndrome, where the nerve passing through the wrist becomes pinched by swollen tissues, and RSI (repetitive strain injuries)., pain and injury associated with repetitive movement. If you suspect you may be suffering from such a condition, have it checked out by a doctor as soon as possible. By the time the pain arrives, you have done some damage to yourself. In my own case, it took eight years for me to develop symptoms. The damage could have been largely prevented if I had been more knowledgeable.

Because journalists and writers are especially prone to these injuries, the National Writers Union (NWU) has taken an active interest in researching and disseminating information to its members. NWU literature on the subject makes the following suggestions:

Take the following symptoms seriously:

- Numbness or pain in one or more fingers.
- Tingling or burning in the hand.
- Shooting pain up the arm.
- Weakness in hands or fingers, trouble buttoning jacket, turning doorknob or gripping objects.
- Pain in forearms, shoulders, neck or back.
- Pain in middle of night or in the morning.

Take the following steps when pain is felt:

- Stop typing.
- Use ice immediately after typing.
- Use ice generally at night before work, or whenever you have pain.
- Use an anti-inflammatory such as ibuprofen to reduce inflammation.
- Rest. You have an injury.

Here are some suggestions to prevent injury and discomfort related to computer work—and prolonged sitting. Please read them carefully and begin incorporating some of them into your daily work routine.

- Warm up your hands before typing. Take frequent rest breaks, get up, walk around move your muscles at least 5 minutes every half-hour to 15 minutes every two hours.
- Sit properly in your chair. Your feet should rest firmly on the floor with the knees slightly higher than the chair seat. Use a footrest if you need to. There should be no pressure on the back side of your leg above and below the knee. Dangling legs strains the lower back muscles and can cut off circulation behind knees. The lower back is supported by chair back. (I use a small pillow, more as a reminder to sit erect.) Forearms should be parallel to the floor.

91

- Use an anti-glare filter on your computer screen.
- Don't slouch at the computer. Keep your head centered above your spine so the neck is not bending forward.
- Hold your wrist flat and on the same plane as your forearm. A flexed or extended wrist causes pressure on the median nerve as you type, which can lead to carpal tunnel syndrome. Avoid bending your wrists up, which can irritate the tendons in your wrists.
- Keep your shoulders relaxed, not hunched.

When I am on a job, I insist on a decent, adjustable chair. Don't be shy about this—it's *your* health and well-being. In addition, there is equipment that you can bring with you, if not provided by the company, that can help you avoid the strain caused by excessive computer use. Check into the following:

- **Document holder.** Documents and screen should be at the same distance from your eyes so you needn't refocus each time you switch between screen and document.
- **Wrist rest** (flat pad to support wrists). I carry a wrist rest with me to every assignment.
- **Track ball mouse.** It's much easier on the wrist than the standard mouse.
- **Wrist brace.** There are special braces you can buy that hold the wrist and hand in the correct position. I use an ace bandage to support my wrist and forearm, and it seems to work well.

There are several special-design keyboards that are supposed to reduce the stress on the hands, wrist and arms. Until they become widely accepted and mass-produced, they will be too expensive for many people. Four that are currently available are:

1. Tony! developed by Anthony Hodges of Mountain View, California, is hinged in the middle, and the center can be raised to move the hands into a more natural thumbs-up position. Hinges allow halves to pivot forward or backward and individual keys can be moved closer together or farther apart to fit user.

2. Comfort keyboard is highly adjustable. It is broken into three units, each one is adjustable in height, pitch and direction. By Health Care Keyboard.

3. Kinesis Corporation has designed a keyboard that relocates the keys from a standard board into two shallow wells a little over six inches apart to allow the arms and wrists to run straight from the shoulder instead of bending the forearm in and the wrist out.

4. Dr. Alan Grant, an optometrist in Chevy Chase, Maryland, has modified the Qwerty keyboard to one with a ridge in the middle, a trackball to control the cursor with the thumbs, and the 12 function keys in a circle like a clock.

There are a number of others under development presently. If you are interested in further information, ask your librarian to help you research them.

In theory, technology is supposed to make the job easier. Too often, the practical application is one of technology increasing its difficulty. Whenever you are on a job, assume the role of outside consultant, observe how the work is produced, see if you can come up with ways to automate portions of it. Use Paul Fox's "Creativity Checklist" in Chapter 5 to figure out how to do it faster and more easily. Use the opportunity that temping gives you—a rare opportunity to have a paid apprenticeship.

Discounted software catalogs

Egghead Discount Software 800-EGGHEAD
800-Software, Inc. 800-888-4880
MacConnection 800-334-4444
PC Connection 800-243-8088

Ergonomic computer aids catalogs

AliMed Inc., 297 High Street, Dedham, MA 02026-9135, 800-225-2610.

Quill Corporation, 717-272-6100.

Further reading

The Secret Guide to Computers, 18th ed., Russ Walters, 22 Ashland Street, Somerville, MA 02144, 617-666-2666.

Peter Norton's PC Problem Solver, Peter Norton, Brady Books, 1993.

The "Dummy" series from I.D.G.:
  DOS for Dummies, Dan Gookin, 1993.
  Windows for Dummies, Andy Rathbone, 1993.
  Macs for Dummies, David Pogue, 1993.

Voodoo Mac, Kay Yarborough Nelson, Ventana Press, 1993

This is the Mac. It's Supposed to be Fun, A. Naiman, J. Kadyk, Peachpit Press, 1993.

Organized to Be the Best, Susan Silver, Adams-Hall, 1991. Has terrific sections about business software and for organizing hard disks for both IBM and Macintosh.

Magazines

PC Magazine, P.O. Box 54093, Boulder, CO 80322, 303-447-9330.

PC Computing, Ziff-Davis Publishing Co., P.O. Box 50253, Boulder, CO 80321-0253, 800-365-2770.

MacGuide Magazine, 444 17th Street, Suite 200, P.O. Box 5937TA, Denver, CO 80217, 800-873-1454.

MacUser, P.O. Box 52461, Boulder, CO 80321-2461, 415-378-5600.

Chapter 7

The Home Office, and the Professional Who Works There

Since the late 1980s, newspapers and magazines have reported how the employee of the future will be a telecommuter located in a home office. At least once a week I see an article about the perils and pluses of telecommuting, dispensing pointers on how to gain recognition though out of sight, or how to keep a career on track while working at home. This leads me to believe that telecommuting's time has come. Whether you intend to make temping a career, use it to subsidize other business interests or as a bridge to a new permanent job that theoretically could evolve into telecommuting, the time for the home office is now.

There are numerous books devoted to all aspects of home offices, including the psychological components of home-based employment. Working in the home office is considerably different than working in a regular office, and I advise you to read as much of these sources as you can, as well as garner tips from other self-employed individuals.

This chapter will touch on some of these factors along with how to economically set up and equip an effective home office. Included at the end of this chapter are several titles you might find helpful.

Zoning laws

As a first step, I recommend a polite inquiry into the zoning laws of your community, rather than risk any unpleasant surprises. Communities vary in their regulation of the home business or office and the enforcement of regulation. Even with ordinances on the books, a large number of communities do not enforce them unless there is a complaint. The most frequent sources of complaints, both legitimate and illegitimate, are neighbors, although I read of an instance where a mail carrier complained because of the volume of mail delivered to a residence.

Twelve years ago, I set up a home office in my former suburban community and I didn't know enough to inquire about regulation. Fortunately, no one complained. Now that I know better, I suggest using an anonymous telephone call to your zoning or building department to find out what laws are on the books, if any permits or licenses are needed, what steps are involved in applying for a variance, then proceed in a way that works for you.

Homeowner's insurance

Check your renter's or homeowner's policy to see if you have adequate coverage for the home office. Usually you need to purchase a rider to your standard policy. This is an inexpensive way to cover small service businesses or professional offices that are not open to the public. These riders have restrictions: that the business does not use more than 20 percent of the residence's square footage, that it involves no unusually high liability risks, excludes the use of flammable chemicals or heavy machinery and has few, if any, employees. Most standard policies specifically exclude some or all of the following:

1. Dwellings that are not used principally as a residence, with *principally* defined as 80 percent or more of the square footage.
2. Separate structures used wholly or in part for business purposes.
3. Business property used to conduct a business on the premises. This includes all home office furnishings and equipment.

4. Inventory or samples used for business and stored at home.
5. Any losses connected with fraudulent use of business credit cards, forged business checks or acceptance of counterfeit money by the business.
6. Electrical surge damage to business equipment or personal use equipment.
7. Personal liability or medical payments for injuries or damage arising from business pursuit or to persons eligible for state worker's compensation benefits or disability.

Taking inventory

At whatever point the office is set up, make a written list of all business equipment and furniture and store in your bank safety deposit box. This list should include such items as a computer or word-processor, printer, fax machine, telephone, answering machine, copier, desk, filing cabinets, shelves and any other electronic equipment or furniture you need to run your home office. This is an important record to have for tax purposes if you are audited (tax considerations are covered in the next chapter), or to prove the value of your investment for casualty loss. The list should include:

• The manufacturer, serial number and special options of all equipment, with attached copies of sales receipts.
• All office furniture with a detailed description, with attached copies of sales receipts.

Organizing and physical space

Not only is every business different, the space available in the home and the working conditions vary. Some entrepreneurs have young children at home, others may live alone with no distractions. Since entire books are devoted to this topic, I will only pass along general tips for a *no-frills*, working office.

1. Set up a functional work area with supplies organized and stored where they can easily be found. Make sure the space is clear of unnecessary items. Organize the area to reduce the amount of time you spend looking for things. Keep

related items together: all computer supplies in one place, all paper in one place, etc. Keep frequently used items close at hand, occasionally used items in desk drawers or a closet, seldom-used items boxed and stored.

2. Set up a filing system that works—and *use* it. A serious contender for the number-one time-waster title is "searching for stuff." Filed material is easily found. Keep frequently used files in your desk or a portable crate while you are using them.

3. Devise a method to keep track of telephone numbers. It doesn't matter what form it takes—rolodex, planner, computer or electronic organizer. If you have to rummage through files or papers constantly to find a number, you're wasting a lot of time.

4. Streamline the way you handle paperwork. Set up systems that help you keep papers moving ahead, whether into a file, the mail or the trash.

5. Organize your business expense receipts with tax time in mind.

6. Keep on hand bank deposit/function slips and certified mail/receipt requested cards and slips.

7. Once a year, purge your files. Go through everything, sorting each item into one of four piles: 1) current, 2) older reference, 3) of historical interest, or 4) unsure. Put the current paper in the front of file, older material in the back of the folder. Store historical materials and place "to-think-about" materials in a folder to look at in a month and decide. Toss the remainder.

8. A clean desk is the sign of an insane, but organized, mind. Only those *work-related* items you use frequently or daily should be *on* your desk. Items you use weekly can go in drawers, monthly on shelves near your desk. Get rid of the decorative items. Let them decorate other surfaces.

9. Sort your mail before opening. I throw away most envelopes with bulk rate postage without ever opening them.

10. Sort paperwork daily into the proper category for quick and efficient handling (mail, completed work from temp folder), using whatever method works for you. Some people use

stacking bins for this. I do better with colored folders labeled with the appropriate categories. Here are several categories that work.

To Do/ Call	Items needing prompt handling, to be added to weekly list.
To Pay	Bills opened, date for payment marked on envelope, extraneous junk inserts tossed.
To Read	Material to read later.
To File	Write where to file it in the upper left-hand corner.

If it's an article or news clip, highlight the important information.

(Have you ever read over a clipping several times and wondered why in the world you saved it? Or, am I the only one who did this before I reformed?)

Decide Later	Paper or articles I can't part with initially. When I look at the material a month later, I often toss it. It helps to keep my information junkie tendencies in check.

Another method that works when I haven't looked through the folder for several months, I take the lower half of the *decide later* pile and throw it away sight unseen.

The Toss Decision	Ask yourself before throwing away: Will I ever refer to it again? Can I find the information elsewhere if I need it? Can I file it in a way that I will find it again easily?

11. Keep an organizer or planner handy. I use a year-at-a-glance wall calendar to track my deadlines and seminar sessions, and a portable planner to carry with me.

12. Receipts sorted in the appropriate categories throughout the year speeds up tax preparation. An easy way to accomplish this is to use an accordion folder with the categories marked in more or less alphabetical order to file receipts. At tax time add up the categories and give the results to your tax person.

Office furniture

The range in quality and price for desks, chairs, file cabinets and computer tables is impressive. Take the time to visit showrooms. Sit in the chairs. Sit at the desks or computer stands. Test these items for ergonomics and comfort. Then, of course, try to get the same piece discounted or on sale.

You might consider shopping for *used* furniture, often advertised in the classifieds, by both individuals, as well as businesses that may be getting rid of perfectly good desks and cabinets because they no longer go with the company's new decor.

Whatever your source, consider these purchases carefully. Even at a "steal," a chair that puts a strain on your back, or a desk that is just two inches too large for your office space is no bargain.

A number of off-price suppliers publish catalogs for those who would like to shop and compare prices from an armchair. A list of furniture and office supplies catalogs can be found at the end of this chapter.

Office supplies

Office supplies can be expensive, many items are grossly over-priced, even from discount catalogues. Follow the same rules as you would with careful grocery shopping:

1. When shopping at a retail outlet, always have a list. To qualify for discounts, buy in *sensible* bulk when possible. Never buy more than you can comfortably store.

2. No matter how tempting, don't buy items because they are on sale. A good buy on items that sit unused for years (taking up valuable storage space) is no bargain.

3. Buy supplies only as needed when you first start out. Try to replenish supplies before running out. Always keep at least

one extra printer ribbon or toner cartridge (or other hard-to-replace items) on hand for emergencies.

4. Reuse and recycle: paper clips, file folders, manila envelopes (use the envelopes for storage or to carry things when you temp, not to send out again.)

5. Use catalogs whenever you can for convenience and home delivery, and to save time and money.

6. When buying stationery and envelopes, check opaqueness. On my first purchase of imprinted envelopes, I found that the contents showed through. The envelopes—1,000 of them—were neither cheap nor returnable.

   Make sure stationery and envelopes aren't too thick for use in laser printers. Also, check that the letterhead can be used in copiers without jamming.

7. Pre-addressed mailing labels imprinted with your business name give a professional appearance and are time-savers. They are sold in lots of 500 or 1,000.

8. Don't be penny wise and pound foolish. Anything going to clients should not look like a bargain. You want to appear professional and to be taken seriously.

Telephones

Install your own telephone with the help of a how-to-do-it book. Take a look at your telephone bill. Get rid of the wire maintenance charge. In the rare event that something goes wrong with your internal wiring, you can fix it yourself or call an electrician.

Get a no-fee telephone credit card for convenience, to use in an emergency, to place calls from pay telephones, or to bypass hotel switchboards.

If you spend a large amount of time on the telephone, buy a headset. It frees your hands for other tasks and is certainly easier on the body than the popular crooked-neck-with-receiver-on-hunched-shoulder position.

When selecting a phone, helpful features to consider are:

- **Hold button.** Putting a caller on hold is more professional than putting a hand over the receiver.
- **Auto-redial.** To redial numbers that are busy.

- More than one line, or **automatic phone mail**, rather than call-waiting.
- **Speaker phone.** Frees you to move about. It is especially useful while you are waiting on hold.

Please refer to Chapter 1, where I discussed answering machines at length.

When considering a long-distance carrier, there are a few factors you should take into account. Are there special discounts for your calling pattern? For example, are most of your long distance business calls during business hours, or the bulk of your calls to the Midwest?

Is the service convenient? Do you have to enter a long dialing sequence to connect to their service? Do they provide a credit card service?

How is the service quality? Are the operators and service representatives easy to reach? Do they have a 24-hour toll-free assistance number for service problems? Is the sound quality good or do voices sound extraterrestrial?

How are the charges figured? What are the rates? For different times of day? For connection?

Check out communications/telephone consultants in your area. They analyze your calling patterns and help you select a cost-effective long-distance service. Their services are provided at no charge to you; they bill the carrier. They are listed in the business classified telephone directories under "Communications Consultants."

New York Telephone has a free service called Home Office Center (800-479-4887). Counselors will help you figure out the appropriate lines or services needed for your home office as well as offer guidance on how to lower your monthly bills. Numerous telephone companies across the country offer similar services, usually under a similar name. Call your local telephone company business office for the referral. For information on discount plans:

AT&T	800-222-0300	US Sprint	800-877-4646
Allnet	800-631-4000	Working Assets	800-788-8588
MCI	800-444-3333		

I have a personal recommendation to make regarding long distance service. I am a Working Assets Long Distance user. I am pleased with the service, the rates run about 10 percent less than other carriers. Every time I use the service, 1 percent of the charge is donated to progressive citizens groups. One day a month, I can make a free "Citizen Call" to legislators about public issues.

Computers

Another benefit from working as a temp is that you are exposed to all kinds of equipment and software. It makes the decision of what to buy for your own office easier. I was able to put off the purchase of a laser printer for a couple of years because I had access to them on most jobs. I became intimately familiar with numerous laser printers. When the time came to buy, I knew which manufacturer and model I wanted. I also knew what I didn't want at any price.

If you are thinking about buying a computer, ask yourself these questions:

1. What do I want to do with the computer? Word processing? Financials? Desktop publishing? (Don't overestimate your needs. The last thing you need is to invest in an expensive system that serves as an over-priced typewriter.

2. How much am I willing to spend? Am I investing in equipment that can be easily upgraded as needed?

3. Is the servicing convenient and affordable?

4. Would it make sense to have a freelancer do whatever work I cannot accomplish during my temporary assignments rather than buy equipment now?

5. If you are shopping for a printer, take along your business letterhead to test for printer handling and printed appearance.

If you know a lot about computers, you might consider mail-order buying. I bought my system that way and have been completely happy with it. If you don't know a lot about computers, become as familiar as possible with the information yourself, but take advantage of a computer-savvy friend when deciding on your purchase.

To conclude this section on computers, I'll share just a few tips from others who learned the hard way.

- Don't be infatuated by those handy all-in-one carts that hold computer, monitor and printer—they save space but can be terribly uncomfortable to work at.

- Magnetic and electrical fields erase data. Don't use magnetic document holders or paperclip holders near the computer. Keep the telephone and electrical cords away as well.

- Surge protectors only work if they are on. Don't use the master switch as an on/off switch. Leave the master switch on, turn computer and monitor off separately.

- Unplug your electronic equipment from wall sockets in a thunderstorm to protect it from power fluctuations too severe for the surge protector.

- Did you know there is compression software that will double your hard disk capacity? I use Stacker software for that purpose, but it does slow down the computer. Your central processing unit (CPU) should be 386 or better to use it.

Cut postage costs and improve mail delivery

Chances are your business efforts will require an increased use of the postal services. The cost for mail delivery continues to go up almost every year. Here are some tips to save time and money.

1. Don't waste time at the post office; buy stamps in bulk or order them by mail at 800-STAMP24. You can call 24 hours a day, seven days a week. You must pay with a credit card. There is a $3 handling charge and it takes three to five days for delivery.

2. There are Postal Business Centers in 150 cities across the country offering free advice on cutting mailing costs. They will update zip codes on your mailing lists to nine-digit numbers to speed up delivery. They even run free seminars for more in-depth information about postal discounts.

3. If you send considerable mail, purchase a postage scale.

4. Use lightweight mailing envelopes without metal clasps. They cost a little more but you will save considerably on postage.

5. The postal service uses optical scanners to sort mail. The service recommends the use of single-spaced uppercase letters, no punctuation in a flush-left block format. The first line of the address should include the city, state (2-letter designation) and ZIP. Do not place the ZIP on a separate line. Here's an example:

MARVIN MARY COMPANY
167 WEST OLIVE BLVD
AKRON OH 82515

6. Because of the scanners, do not use dark-colored envelopes or labels, ornate or hard-to-read typefaces, or envelopes cluttered with advertising.
7. Keep on hand to fill out ahead of time, forms for certified mail, express mail and any courier service you might use.

Working at home: A dream or a nightmare?

Most books on home offices or self-employment mention the psychological factors of working at home. It takes a certain amount of discipline to work for yourself and keep your personal and business lives separated. Working as a temp can ease the transition period for those of you who are trying self-employment for the first time. Let me offer four simple suggestions on how to keep your business and personal lives separate for those times you are working in a home office.

- Set business hours and work during those times.
- Let your answering machine screen calls until you have educated friends not to call you during business hours.
- Keep to-do lists for personal items separate from *business* to-do lists. If you have "pick up dry cleaning" and "get oil changed" on the same list as "reorganize files" and "complete weekly sales report," you're headed for trouble.
- Schedule activities with friends at least once a week to avoid becoming a lonely workaholic.

There is no set formula for any of this. One of the biggest mistakes people make in setting up a home office is to copy what they had in a corporation. However you set up your office, combine your job search

105

with consulting projects or temp full-time, remember, you're the designer. It can be anything you want it to.

For further reading

Conquering the Paper Pile-Up, Stephanie Culp, Writer's Digest Books, 1990.

How to File and Find It, free booklet from Quill Corporation, Business Library, 100 Shelter Road, Lincolnshire, IL 60069.

Organizing Your Home Office for Success, Lisa Kanarek, Penguin Group, 1993.

The Complete Work-At-Home Companion, Herman Holtz, Prima Publishing, 1990.

Organized to Be the Best, Susan Silver, Adams-Hall Publishing, 1991.

Office at Home, Robert Scott, Scribner, 1985.

The Phone Book, a Consumer Reports Book by Carl Oppendahl. How to choose, fix and install equipment and everything you should know about getting the best service at the lowest cost.

Complete Guide to Lower Phone Costs, Consumers Checkbook, 1984.

Catalogs

Planning items

Caddylak Systems
510 Fillmore Avenue
Tonawanda, NY 14150
800-523-8060

Discounted office furniture

National Business Furniture, Inc.
222 East Michigan Street
Milwaukee, WI 53202
414-276-8511

Office Furniture Center
322 Moody Street, Dept. 6001
Waltham, MA 02154
617-893-7300

Factory Direct Furniture
225 East Michigan St., Suite 11
Milwaukee, WI 53202-4900
414-289-9770

Frank Eastern Co.
599 Broadway
New York, NY 10012-3258
212-219-0007

Discounted office supplies

Quill Corporation
P.O. Box 1450
Lebanon, PA 17042-1450
717-272-6100 (customer service—all regions: 708-634-8000)
  I have dealt with Quill for about 10 years. They continually have the lowest prices for the items I use, and their service is terrific.

Staples, Inc.
P.O. Box 9328
Framingham, MA 01701-9328
508-370-8500

Viking Office Products
800-735-4000

Schiller & Schmidt, Inc.
800-621-1503

Reliable Office Supply
800-421-1222

Phar-Mor Corp.
800-522-5444

Hello Direct (telephone products)   800-444-3556
Hold Everything (organizing supplies)   800 421-2264

Discounted computer supplies

Lyben Computer Systems
313-649-2500

MacConnection
800-334-4444

PC Connection
800-243-8088

800-Software, Inc.
800-888-4880

MEI/Micro Center
800-634-3478

Dartek (Macintosh)
708-832-2100

Consumer group
Telecommunications Research and Action Center (TRAC)
P.O. Box 12038
Washington, DC 20005
202-462-2520
  A nonprofit consumer advocacy and educational organization that provides information on services and prices of long distance carriers to its members.

C hapter 8

Temping for
Supplemental Income

This recession/depression of the late 1980s, early 1990s has changed the definition of work for many Americans. No longer is a job defined by its title, but by the skill it takes to complete it. If we are to believe the press, the new "career path" will be simultaneous multiple jobs and the management of multiple relationships—free agents selling their skills to solve problems across industry lines.

As an individual exploring the world of temporary work, you are on the crest of this work force wave of the future. Whether you are using temporary work as a way to supplement your income, to fund a home-based or other new business, or to embark upon a career of free-lance and agency temping, you are indeed a free agent selling your skills and juggling multiple professional relationships.

To do so successfully, you must immediately begin to perceive yourself as a self-employed professional, an entrepreneur, the president of your own enterprise—then to set up your business and position yourself accordingly. This chapter will explore three ways to utilize temporary employment: as an income subsidy for a new business/consulting startup, as an important part of a job search for permanent employment or as a full-time occupation, combining working for agencies and freelancing.

Before leaving full-time employment

If you are still employed full-time, you have an opportunity to get a head start. Self-employment, whatever form it takes, should be a planned sequence of events. However, the first thing I want to emphasize is: *Everything will take twice as long as you think it will and will cost considerably more.* The more information you can gather, the more planning you can do, the more pitfalls you can avoid, the better chance you will have of success. Here are 19 things you can do while you are still getting a paycheck.

1. Talk to people who are in business for themselves, preferably a similar business to the one you're planning: What were some of their problems, their surprises? What did they wish they had done first? What would they have done differently? What advice would they give you?

2. Expand your present credit lines, apply for cards you don't have while you are still employed. It's a lot more complicated to expand your credit once you are self-employed.

3. Find out about professional and support organizations and begin to attend meetings. When you become self-employed, the nature of your former business friendships will change. Your life will be quite different from friends who work for a company. It is important to begin making the acquaintance of other entrepreneurs like yourself.

4. Think about office space and supplies:
   - If you expect to lease space, start looking at potential areas and sites as well as making contacts.
   - If you plan to work at home, get graph paper and play with room and furniture arrangements, or start moving furniture around to give yourself space.
   - Buy a desk, chair, file cabinet, office supplies (only items you are sure you will use). Rarely do you fully appreciate

how expensive these items are until you need them all at once.

- • If your employer places large stationery orders, perhaps you can add on some items for yourself and take advantage of their volume discount. That, of course, will depend on your relationship with the company or supplier.

5. Join professional organizations at company expense where memberships will benefit you and will still be good when you resign. Take pertinent company or company-reimbursed training courses wherever possible.

6. Subscribe to magazines at company expense where appropriate. Make use of corporate libraries and company time to research your industry and markets.

7. Determine which business entity is best for your business: sole proprietorship; partnership; corporation; s corporation. The public libraries are full of books with lengthy definitions of these entities as well as lists of their advantages and disadvantages.

8. Acquire or hone your financial skills by reading some of magazines that offer general advice on popular financial topics. Most libraries subscribe to several and the librarian can direct you. Two to get you started are *Money* and *Kiplinger's Personal Finance.*

9. Send away for free financial publications (addresses and/or telephone numbers are at chapter's end). *How to Read a Financial Report*, Merrill Lynch; *Guide to Financial Instruments*, Coopers & Lybrand; *How to Read The Wall Street Journal*, The Wall Street Journal; *Take Charge of Your Money*, AARP. For government consumer publications, write for a listing from the Consumer Information Center.

10. Talk to your accountant or tax person about the financial implications of self-employment. Set up a simple system to log your tax-deductible expenses. If you don't know how to do this kind of thing, now is time to learn.

11. Talk to your insurance person. Find out what insurance is appropriate to your business and what the cost will be. If you decide to make any changes, obtain and complete

application forms. Don't overlook medical and disability coverage for yourself.

12. Choose a name for your business. You will be surprised how much time and thought this involves. The name will be influenced by your business entity. For instance, sole proprietorships cannot use "Associates" in the name.

13. Register your business name with the county clerk and get your DBA (doing business as) certificate. Take care of the required name search. Some states require you to publish an official notice of your intention to do business as well.

14. If your business service or products are taxable, or you will need additional licenses or permits (in addition to the DBA), complete the appropriate paperwork and get the process underway.

15. Query the local zoning board or building department anonymously about community residential or zoning regulations that affect home offices.

16. Get stationery and business cards once you have chosen a name. This will give you an opportunity to do some price comparisons with printers. Consider bartering services or, if you're lucky, maybe a printer you know through your present job will do you a favor. Most large stationery stores have sample letterhead and business cards so you can start getting some ideas of what you might want for yourself.

17. Start compiling a list of all business friends and contacts, personal friends you will want to notify at the appropriate time that you are in business. This will take time and should be an ongoing project.

18. Use up remaining sick time before leaving a salaried job by having elective surgery or a medical procedure you have been putting off. Get it taken care of while you still have comprehensive medical insurance and accumulated sick days.

19. Set deadlines or target dates. Keep a log of what you've accomplished. Otherwise, you are going to feel that nothing is being accomplished—the more you do, the more there is to do.

Freelance temping/consulting

Some temps prefer to skip the agency connection and deal directly with the client. The biggest benefit is in the money. Given the 40-percent to 50-percent agency markup, a freelance temp can get a much higher hourly rate, and the client can save money.

What services do agencies perform for that 40 percent to 50 percent? They drum up the business and serve as booking agents. They pay their temps weekly, waiting 30, 90 or 120 days for companies to pay them. If the company never pays, the temp is still paid. The agency check doesn't bounce. (Well, rarely, anyway.) They pay one-half of the temp's Social Security "contribution." They pay into worker's compensation, state disability and unemployment funds.

If you are new to temporary employment, I recommend working through an agency while you learn the ropes (the paid apprenticeship). Get some experience under your belt before branching out on your own.

Business cards. The more professional you look, the easier it will be to convince potential clients to hire you. Every successful freelance temp I talked to agreed you must have business cards printed. Stationery stores and quick-print shops have a wide-range of samples in different layouts, typeface, and prices for you to examine. At any rate, the information you need to include is: name, telephone, message telephone if it is different, and what it is that you do.

Taxes. Talk to your tax preparer about the tax benefits and deductions in running your own freelance business. From the beginning set up your business records the right way. Put in place some process to handle receipts, a notebook to record mileage in your car, if appropriate, and so forth.

Along with tax benefits come certain responsibilities, such as filing quarterly estimated tax returns. It takes discipline to put a fixed amount of money into an interest-bearing account designated for taxes—but you are getting the interest, not the government. Remember, those weekly deductions agencies take don't go to the government; they go into an interest-bearing account for the agency until the quarterly filing deadline.

112

Take the necessary steps to establish your enterprise as a legitimate business. If a sole proprietorship seems to be the appropriate business entity for your efforts, get a DBA certificate, obtainable in county offices for a modest sum (range is $10 to $50). It makes your business records and income discernable from your personal ones for tax purposes. Later down the road, you might want to get a tax I.D. and/or a separate business checking account as well.

Read Chapters 9 and 10 for more detailed information on taxes and insurance. Chapter 7 has tips for the home office.

Jury duty. The federal court system as well as most state courts are unsympathetic to temps asking to be excused for financial reasons. The court system is impervious to the fact that no one can live on the $15 per day they pay jurors. However, temps who have a DBA certificate and are sole proprietors will be excused without difficulty.

Tips for finding clients. Look through the permanent employment classified ads for positions where your skill and experience would be a good match. Call the companies to offer your temporary services while they search for the "right person" for the job.

Nonprofit organizations need additional people during their fund drives. Find out what the drives are, when they are held, who is in charge of staffing them and offer your services.

Consider running a "Situations Wanted" advertisement in one of the trade papers. Read current ads. Call the people advertising their services and ask what kind of response they have had. Look in the library at various papers if you don't know where to advertise.

If you do decide to run an ad, and your services are word processing/secretarial, have it appear for Thursday's paper. Office managers begin thinking about staffing for the next week at this point. All ads should mention being paid on a per-day basis. You want to be paid at the end of the day on a short assignment, not 60 days later.

Research the seasonal needs or the likely special projects of specific industries or individual companies. Make direct contact with those in charge if you can, rather than through personnel departments. Local papers often furnish leads in their announcements of whom is heading up which fund raiser or flavor-of-the-month event.

Numerous large companies maintain their own temp work force. Query personnel departments directly. You will receive a higher hourly rate than agencies, but less than if you freelance your services.

Use the prospecting technique that agency sales reps use: making cold calls to all the offices in a building. You can try chatting with the receptionist to get the name of the correct person to contact. Sometimes it is possible to briefly talk with the person. You can always leave your business card with the receptionist.

If you have a specialty, work for specialty agencies for awhile to get a feel for the type of projects temps are used for.

Don't pirate clients from your agencies. Follow the temporary services contract to the letter as well as in spirit.

Setting rates. Make sure that the client understands you want to be paid at the end of the day for a one-day assignment. When you work for a week, request a check by noon on Friday. Take the check to their bank and cash it on your lunch hour.

Don't quote a rate until you find out what is involved in the job. If someone is insistent, give a range. Your rate will be more than an agency would pay you, but less than the agency would bill the client, plus Social Security contribution and expenses. Specific instructions on how to figure rates is in Chapter 9.

Exercises and tools for the competitive edge

Let's say you have come up with a great idea for a service or business. Unless you specifically define *what you want to do* and *how you intend to go about doing it,* your "business" or your "consulting service" will remain an idea rattling around in your head.

The feasibility exercise following will be a valuable assistance in determining whether your idea can be turned into a viable, money-making business. It also helps existing new consulting businesses to define their issues and problems. For the best results, write out the answers. Committing your thoughts and strategies to paper makes them more concrete.

Feasibility exercise

The business itself

1. *What will the business do? What do you want to do with it?*

Suppose you want to set up a consulting business in your specialty, which is sales training. What areas of sales would that be? Why not every area you can think of? Do you want to do this in your home town? Nationwide? Will you train beginners? Managers only?

2. *What form of organization will you use? Why?*

   Three of your former business associates and you have discussed an alliance, possibly a partnership. How would this best be set up if you decide to go this route? Or, you have decided you don't want partners. What were the factors in reaching that decision? The forms of organization most frequently used for small businesses are: sole proprietorship, partnership, limited partnership and sub-chapter "s" corporation.

3. *What would your roles be if you ally yourself with another consultant?*

   How would decisions be reached? Who would measure the performance crucial for business success? What would you expect the contribution to be in terms of time, money, talent or experience? Will you also have professional and creative advisers? Who will they be?

Marketing your services

1. *Who/what is the general market for your service? What is your specific market?*

   Define the geographic limits as well as specific types of persons or firms to whom you will sell. For example, your services may benefit the business market. Will you target the manager-level employee? Which companies? What are the titles of persons who will retain your services as well as identities of persons you will train?

2. *What makes you think you can do it better?*

   Distinguish your service from similar ones. How is your training different from others? Xerox Corporation has a widely known sales training program. What can you do that Xerox can't do?

The competition

1. *List the direct competition.* Do your homework. Find out who this is and how and where they operate.

2. *List the indirect competition.* What are related services that could, in theory, perform the same functions you intend to. What about self-help books?

3. *How will you beat the competition?* Quality? Service? Design? Delivery? Filling individual clients' needs? List the specific steps you will take to do it better than anyone else.

Selling, advertising, promotion and public relations

A. Selling.
How will you develop leads and select targets? What will be your sales approach? Your sales tools? Who will develop them? Who will do the actual one-on-one selling? Follow-through? How will you keep clients?

B. Advertising/promotion.
What is your objective? Who is your audience? What is the message? Which media? Frequency? How will you monitor results?

C. Public relations.
Will you use personal appearances? Speeches? Interviews with publications? Public service? Will you write articles or books?

To give yourself ideas, use the following list of "35 Ways to Get Business." (From *Making It On Your Own*, Sarah and Paul Edwards.) I highly recommend reading their book.

Public Relations

Writing articles
Letters to the editor
News releases
Speeches and seminars
Publicity: newspaper,
    magazine, radio,
      TV, business/
      trade publications
Product packaging
Point-of-sale display

Word-of-Mouth

Networking
Mentors and gatekeepers
Volunteerism
Sponsorships
Charitable donations
Referrals
Business name
Letterhead/business card

Direct Marketing

Sampling
Incentives
Discount pricing
Contests/giveaways
Newsletters
Circulars/flyers
Trade shows/exhibits
Sales seminars
Demonstrations
Direct mail

Inventive Advertising

Classified ads
Business directories
Yellow pages
Bulletin boards/tear pads
Your own radio show
Your own TV show
Online networking
Fax
Direct-response ads
Card decks

Expenses

Before you can do financial projections and budgets, you will need to track your expenses. On the following two pages are forms I found helpful in getting a handle on expenses.

Where to look for low-cost counseling

American Woman's Economic Development Corporation (AWED). AWED is a nonprofit corporation dedicated to helping women become successful entrepreneurs. It runs low-cost programs underwritten by both public and private sectors. Several years ago, I went through one of their courses, "Starting Your Own Business." Forty-five of us started together, only 15 finished. It helped to clarify whether we really wanted to be in business for ourselves. Tackling the realities of doing a business plan for nebulous ideas, and some actual financial forecasting, helped us to be more realistic. AWED has now added help in securing financing.

Currently, under a $1 million matching grant from the Small Business Administration, AWED has established regional centers in Washington, D.C., and Los Angeles. (For more information, contact AWED at 71 Vanderbilt Avenue, New York, NY 10169, 212-692-9009 or 800-321-6962.)

Temp By Choice

Monthly Expense Checklist	Estimated	Actual	Yearly
Office rent (or portion of home)	_____	_____	_____
Printing/supplies not paid by clients	_____	_____	_____
Equipment (monthly payment or savings for future cash purchases)	_____	_____	_____
Tax return preparation, other accounting expenses	_____	_____	_____
Legal services (projected, prorated)	_____	_____	_____
Typing, secretarial services	_____	_____	_____
Telephone	_____	_____	_____
Utilities (percent in home)	_____	_____	_____
Insurance costs (projected, prorated)	_____	_____	_____
Retirement contribution	_____	_____	_____
Savings (business, personal)	_____	_____	_____
Loan payment	_____	_____	_____
Taxes (FICA or pension plan)	_____	_____	_____
License renewal	_____	_____	_____
Answering service	_____	_____	_____
Subscriptions	_____	_____	_____
Books, reference material	_____	_____	_____
Marketing	_____	_____	_____
Entertainment, promotion	_____	_____	_____
Advertising	_____	_____	_____
Automobile	_____	_____	_____
Travel (in town, out of town)	_____	_____	_____
Professional development	_____	_____	_____
Salary (must be large enough to meet personal expenses)	_____	_____	_____
Miscellaneous	_____	_____	_____

Monthly Personal Expense Detail	Estimated	Actual	Yearly
Rent/Mortgage	___	___	___
Food	___	___	___
Telephone	___	___	___
Medical (OV, medication)	___	___	___
Medical Insurance	___	___	___
Car	___	___	___
Renters/Homeowners insurance	___	___	___
Disability insurance	___	___	___
Electricity	___	___	___
Clothing	___	___	___
Entertainment	___	___	___
Haircuts, cleaners	___	___	___
Dental	___	___	___
Investments	___	___	___

There are other sources of assistance and counseling as well.

- Entrepreneurial Centers connected with local colleges.
- SCORE or other SBA-sponsored groups. Call 800-827-5722 for services, videos and publications.
- Chambers of commerce often sponsor or subsidize training.
- Local business press/newsletters, and small business columns.

Temping combined with a job search

Let temporary employment help you get the information you need to narrow your job search. Tell your agencies what you are looking for.

Temp By Choice

Use the temp assignment itself to assist you in accomplishing your goals. On the job, explore, ask questions, read their literature, let it be known that you have other skills and interests.

Do your homework.

1. What new industries interest you to explore as a possible change?

2. Are there related fields that would enhance your present career that are worth gaining experience in?

3. What about growing fields worth looking at? Check the U.S. Labor Department's Occupational Outlook Quarterly.

4. Are there companies or industries where you could pick up useful information, helpful contacts or applicable skills?

Use the telephone. If there are companies or industries you want to explore, call their personnel departments. Ask which temporary employment agencies they use, then sign up with the agencies. Tell the agency you are particularly interested in working for the company/industry.

Inform agencies of your interests. Make it a point to communicate to each of your counselors the specific companies and industries you are interested in.

Utilize specialty agencies. Talk to specialty agencies about your areas of expertise, but don't discount the general agencies, especially ones that have long-term relationships with their client companies. They fill a variety of jobs for their clients and can get a specialized rate for you. If you are not knowledgeable about temporary opportunities in your field, interview with one or two specialty agencies. Let them assess your skills. Learn if you have gaps in your knowledge or skills that you need to do something about.

This will also work if you want to break into a new field. Talk to the specialty agencies. Find out what training/knowledge/skills are required to work for them. Then, go out and get them.

12 things you can find out on a temp assignment

1. How do the people relate to each other. Do they work alone or in groups?
2. Is there an air of frenzy with many people chasing their tails over contrived busy work?
3. Are employees relaxed and casual? Stiff and formal? Quiet and fearful?
4. Are there minorities and women in upper management? Their numbers and placement tell you a great deal about salary structure and advancement opportunities in the company.
5. Is there a lot of turnover? Does the company seem to have mostly new, temporary employees in support and administrative positions? Why?
6. What type of employee is most valued? College graduates? Company-experienced? Docile? Feisty?
7. What are the company's major products and services? Who are the company's customers?
8. How do competitors and customers view the company's services or products? Excellent? Shoddy?
9. What are some of the company's recent success stories? What do they tell you about the company's definition of success?
10. Is the company publicly owned? Privately owned? Part of larger conglomerate? What is its relationship with the parent company?
11. Has the company declined or grown over the past five years? How many employees have been laid off?
12. How is the morale of the remaining core employees?

Spruce up your act

Here are three ways to refurbish the presentation of your skill and experience to others. Get visual and audio feedback on how you perform on interviews. Have practice interviews videotaped. Use your tape recorder to record practice interviews. Rework your resume.

Temp By Choice

Classified ads draw hundreds, sometimes thousands of responses and often these responses sit in piles on desks. Try to circumvent personnel departments whenever possible. As a temp, I have seen first-hand such resume piles. Sometimes I have been the one who opens the mail and makes the first cut.

Resumes. The resume tells lot about you. It is a visual picture of who you are. It must be pleasing to the eye, contain the pertinent information succinctly and be error-free. One of the best books I found on shaping the resume is *The Smart Woman's Guide to Resumes and Job Hunting* (by Julie King and Betsy Sheldon, Career Press, 1993.) The resume proofread checklist is quoted with permission.

Final proofread checklist

1. Spell-check your resume if you are using a computer.
2. Read it aloud, preferably with another person reading silently with you.
3. Read it backwards. You will focus on individual words rather than the meaning of phrases or sentences.
4. Ask someone else to proofread it. In fact, get as much feedback as possible from people who will tell you the truth.

Brave new world

At the end of 1993 there were as many unemployed white-collar workers in America as there were unemployed blue-collar workers. These are educated, middle-class women and men whose jobs have been eliminated. Their jobs will not be coming back. So many companies are using temporary workers by whatever label...contract workers, consultants, project workers, temps...that a mixed work force is no longer considered an exotic exception. The business language itself is beginning to reflect this trend. A number of agencies are now calling themselves "providers of interim workers" in an effort to minimize any stigma attached to the word "temp." Companies are referring to their permanent employees as "core," and their garden-variety temporary workers as "contingent."

With your goals firmly in mind, wherever you fit into this picture, go out now into this brave new world and use temporary employment to your advantage.

For further reading

The Complete Work-At-Home Companion, Herman Holtz, Prima Publishing, 1990.

Making It On Your Own: Surviving and Thriving on the Ups and Downs of Being Your Own Boss, Sarah and Paul Edwards, St. Martin's Press, 1991.

The Entrepreneur's Ultimate Resource Book, The Entrepreneurial Center, Inc., 1993.

The Home Office and Small Business Answer Book, Janet Attard, Henry Holt, 1993.

Self-employment: Career Press

Breakaway Careers, The Self-Employment Resource for Freelancers, Consultants and Corporate Refugees, Bill Radin, 1994.

Start Up, An Entrepreneur's Guide to Launching and Managing a New Business, 3rd edition, William J. Stolze, 1994.

Job search/career: Career Press

The Smart Woman's Guide to Resumes and Job Hunting, 2nd edition, Julie Adair King and Betsy Sheldon, 1993.

The Smart Woman's Guide to Interviewing and Salary Negotiation, Julie Adair King, 1993.

Thriving in Tough Times, Paul G. Fox, 1992.

Adventure Careers, Alex Hiam & Susan Angle, 1992.

Take This Job and Leave It, Bill Radin, 1993.

Part-Time Careers, Joyce Hadley, 1993.

101 Great Answers to the Toughest Interview Questions, Ron Fry, 1994.

The Cover Letter Book, Richard Fein, 1994.

Finding a Job After 50, Terry Harty and Karen K. Harty, 1994.

Successful ReCareering, Joyce A. Schwarz, 1994.

Business Letters for Busy People, Jim Dugger, 1994.

Thriving in Tough Times, Paul G. Fox, 1992.

Order free publications

How to Read a Financial Report, Merrill Lynch brochure line, 800-637-7455.

Guide to Financial Instruments, Coopers & Lybrand, 1251 Avenue of the Americas, New York, NY 10020, 212-536-2000.

How to Read The Wall Street Journal, The Wall Street Journal, Education Services Bureau, 609-520-4254.

Take Charge of Your Money, AARP, P.O. Box 2240, Long Beach, CA 90801.

Money Matters and the Temp

∙∙

I'm told there is a Chinese curse that says, "May you live in interesting times." And Confucius is to have said, "They must often change who would be constant in happiness or wisdom." Temporary work certainly provides change, and frequent "interesting times." There's probably a message here; those who engage in temp work are smart, happy and cursed.

One of the biggest changes that will take place for those of you who are new to temping is the adjustment to a skill-based mentality, hourly wages, a fluctuating income and, consequently, how you will now control and manage this income. In these times of change, there are opportunities to examine settled-in patterns of behavior, and find better ways to do things we haven't thought about in years—changing banks, investigating low interest-rate credit cards, and so forth.

Income from temping agencies

Temps are paid an hourly wage with time-and-a-half over 40 hours. Evening shifts and weekend work pay more. The agency bills clients 30 percent to 50 percent over the rate it pays temps. The industry standard is a 40-percent to 50-percent markup.

For instance, if you are a word processor in New York City, working second shift (5:30 to midnight), you might earn between $17 and $22 per hour. The agency will bill the client between $25.50 and $33. Temps working on weekends and holidays are generally paid $19 to $24 hourly. Holiday pay applies *only* if the company is closed on that day. The new "floating" holidays make it more difficult to get higher rates.

It is not easy to get one of these later shifts because the companies usually ask for temps by name. I'm convinced actors hand these jobs down from one generation to another. As with so many things, however, perseverance pays off.

Temps successful at capturing these jobs list themselves "available" with dreary persistence until they are finally called. Eventually, one evening all of the client company's favorite workers will be unavailable, and the persistent temp (you) will be called. Thereafter, you will be known to the client. The client will ask for *you* by name.

1. Computation of overtime. If you work over 40 hours for one agency, you must be paid time-and-a-half for those hours, even if you work for different companies. If you work at several different rates of pay, an average or base rate is figured for your overtime pay.

For example, suppose you worked a 46-hour week that breaks down as follows.

20 hours at $15 an hour
10 hours at $17 an hour
8 hours at $20 an hour
8 hours at $14 an hour

The base rate for the six hours of overtime is determined by:

1. Adding the rates ($15 + $17 + $20 + $14 = $66)
2. Dividing the sum ($66) by the number of rates (4). ($66/4 = $16.50)
3. The answer, $16.50, will be the base rate. The base rate is multiplied by 1 and one-half to get the hourly overtime rate. ($16.50 x 1 1/2 = $24.75) The six hours of overtime will be paid at this rate. (6 x $24.75 = $148.50.)

2. Check for paycheck errors. While it is nice to have a weekly paycheck, it brings with it more paperwork to look after. Every agency that I have worked for has made at least one error in my paycheck. No one tried to cheat me; they have personnel problems too. Multiply that probability of error times the number of agencies you work for. Get into the habit of checking your pay stub to verify the accuracy of each of these categories:

- Hourly rate
- Number of hours
- Overtime base rate
- Overtime paid at time-and-a-half

3. Paychecks by mail. Most timesheets have a box to check if you want to receive your paycheck by mail. Often the boxes are small and easily overlooked. Call attention to the mailing instructions with a bright highlighter or a post-it note. Telephone the agency on payday to make sure that the check has, indeed, been mailed.

Keep in mind that if a paycheck is "lost" in the mail, the agency will put a stop payment on it. It will have to clear the bank (another three days) before a replacement check is issued. If that happens to you, immediately verify the address the check was sent to. At least you'll avoid waiting for the check's delayed arrival. As I learned, someone doing data entry work can mess up an address by mistake.

4. Cashing paychecks. Not all agencies provide free check-cashing services. Take the check to the bank it is drawn on and it should be cashed at no charge. Most agencies use nearby banks, one or two blocks away.

Setting freelance rates for temporary work

If you're offering your services as a freelance temp, bypassing agency involvement, then you need to come up with an attractive rate for the client that is less than an agency would charge, yet will net *you* more than an agency would pay. You need to factor in an equitable rate for the skills required and your expenses (including extra commuting time and FICA), to come up with a non-exploitive rate. Don't accept a secretarial rate to do computer consulting or financials.

Let's say an agency rate paid to temps for an uncomplicated secretarial assignment is $16 per hour, plus FICA. The agency would bill the client for $24. Factoring in the longer commute (time is money) and FICA, I would set the freelance rate at $22 per hour for a corporation, $19.50 per hour for a nonprofit organization, only because they pay less as a rule.

Negotiate that you'll receive payment for the work at the end of the day for a one-day assignment, or at noon on Friday for a weeklong assignment. Cash the check immediately at the branch it is drawn on, usually nearby. The check is good 99 percent of the time. However, if there is a problem with the company, you will find out immediately.

Hourly rates for consulting services

You may feel that freelance temp or consulting work may not be worth it to you if you can't earn a certain amount per year. In order to figure out your hourly rate with an annual salary in mind, here is a method of determining such a rate. Let's say you want to make $50,000 next year.

1. 40 hours a week x 52 weeks = 2,080 available hours.
   $50,000 ÷ 2,080 hours = $24.03 per hour

2. Deduct from that: 4 weeks vacation and 3 weeks administrative work (7 weeks, or 280 hours.) Now your earning base is 1,800 hours (45 weeks).
   $50,000 ÷ 1,800 hours = $27.78 per hour

3. Drumming up business may take 25 percent of your time. This reduces the earning base of billable hours to 33.75 weeks or 1,350 hours.
   $50,000 ÷ 1,350 hours = $37.03 per hour

4. Personal benefits (pension, insurance) is about 30 percent of your salary, which means you now have to earn $65,000 (30 percent of $50,000 is $15,000, and $15,000 plus $50,000 is $65,000).
   $65,000 ÷ 1,350 hours = $48.14 per hour

5. Office expenses (equipment, supplies, rent—at least $100 monthly, even if you work out of your home, $200 secretarial help) estimated at $400 per month or $4,800. Add to $65,000.

$69,800 ÷ 1,350 hours = $51.70 per hour

6. Profit: 15 percent before taxes brings total to $74,750 or $55.37 per hour.

Round it off to $60 per hour.

Getting your personal financial picture into focus

The people attending my seminars come from many parts of the employment spectrum. Some are professionals who've been squeezed out of their jobs, some are career-changers, some are women who are reentering the work force because children have begun elementary school or college. They are people with various levels of skill and experience.

Yet, I've discovered that almost all of them, as they made their first steps into a new career direction, were uncertain and insecure about basic financial skills as they related to a variable income—from budgeting and bill-paying to credit and collection. In this chapter, I will touch on their most frequently expressed concerns, assuming that they are likely yours as well.

1. Determining your net worth

Net worth is simply the difference between what you *own* and what you *owe*. Knowing how to figure your net worth is useful in a number of ways. You will need to know it for financial projections if you are thinking of going into business, if you are planning to borrow money or if you are finally getting around to consulting a financial expert for some guidance.

Especially when you are pursuing temp employment because you've been out of work, you're just starting to build up temp work and a steady stream of income is an uncertainty, or using temp work to supplement a startup or home-based business, knowing your net worth is crucial to making any financial decisions.

Here is a quick way for you to figure your net worth from *If Time Is Money, No Wonder I'm Not Rich,* by Mary Sprouse. First, add up your assets:

Liquid assets
1. Cash and cash equivalent assets (bank accounts, money market accounts, CDs, T-bills, employee savings plans).
2. Stocks, bonds and mutual funds.

Nonliquid assets
3. Retirement funds (IRAs, KEOGHs, 401k) and other company plans.
4. Real estate (value of your home, second home, rental property, land, limited partnerships).
5. Cash value of life insurance and annuities.
6. Collectibles (art, antiques, stamps, precious metals).
7. Personal property (cars, furniture, jewelry).
8. Total assets (add lines 3 through 7).

Next, identify and add up your liabilities.

Liabilities
1. Unpaid bills (mortgage or rent, income and property taxes, alimony/child support, medical).
2. Credit card/charge account balances.
3. Loans (mortgages, home equity, car, education, margin account).

Finally, subtract your total liabilities from your assets. That is your net worth.

2. Better banking

All banks and banking services are not equal—particularly for the temp who juggles several agencies and has varying schedules and work locations. If you are planning to change banks in the near future, take the time to evaluate several. Here's what to look for:

1. Check for long lines at the times it is convenient for you to bank.

2. Find out the amount required for opening an account, as well as the minimum balance.
3. How long is the waiting period for funds to be available (cash, local bank checks, same-state or out-of-state banks)?
4. Get a list of fees for: stop payments, bounced checks, monthly service charges and ATM transactions.
5. Look for conveniently located branches and ATMs.
6. Check the bank's policy on third-party checks: Will it accept for deposit?

Check your bank's financial rating with Veribanc, an independent bank-rating firm. In 1992, I had the dubious pleasure of having my checking and savings accounts in a bank that failed. Trust me when I tell you to do everything you can to avoid this experience. The Federal Deposit Insurance Corporation predicted 100 bank failures for 1993, the *lowest* since 1984. No bank with Veribanc's top "Blue Ribbon" recognition has ever failed. Veribanc can be reached at 800-837-4226. There is a modest charge for this information.

Take advantage of the competition between banks to get a no-frills *separate checking* for your business expenses. It doesn't have to be a commercial (in other words, expensive) account. I have two personal accounts, one I use for business only. The checks for that account are printed with my name, then my company name and address. It makes bookkeeping and tax records easier to maintain. A benefit of a separate account is if the IRS audits your business tax returns, the investigator will look solely at the business checks. If your business expenses are mixed in with a personal account, the investigator will delve into everything.

One caution, however: Banks can be sticky about accepting checks endorsed to your business. Most want checks made out to you, rather than your business, for a personal account.

Most banks charge a premium price for their checks. There are several mail order firms that print checks for a modest fee.

Checks in the Mail, Inc.	800-733-4443
Current	800-533-3973
Custom Direct	800-272-5432
Artistic Checks	800-224-7621
The Check Gallery	800-354-3540

3. Getting loans or credit while temping

What happens to your credit rating when you temp? Nothing special. Unless, of course, you go on a wild spending spree or cease paying your creditors.

However, if you are considering applying for a loan or a larger line of credit, the time to do so is while you are still employed full-time. Once you change jobs, or go into business for yourself, banks get nervous, especially in a stalled economy. In fact, there are at least seven things banks hate seeing on credit applications:

1. New businesses.
2. Unemployment at time of application.
3. Self-employed people working out of their homes.
4. Employment with small, unknown (unstable) firms.
5. People of modest income with several revolving accounts, even if their present balance is zero.
6. Using a P.O. Box for an address.
7. No telephone number, or telephone not listed in applicant's name.

4. Choosing economical credit cards

Have you given much thought recently to what your credit cards may be costing you in overpriced charges for their services? How do you evaluate the terms of credit cards? One of the basic ways is how the interest is figured on revolving amounts. Revolving credit is an open-ended credit agreement where you have not agreed to borrow a specific, preset amount and you are permitted a wide range of latitude in repayment. The most consumer-friendly is the *adjusted balance method* (all payments and returns are credited to your account before charging you the monthly interest), followed by the *average daily balance method* (the daily balances are added up and divided by the number of days in the billing period). Other factors in an economical selection should include:

- Low interest rate
- No or low yearly fee

- Grace period. Most cards allow 20 to 30 days before the bill is paid to start charging interest. However, some begin charging interest the minute the charge is made.
- Low late fees or penalties

Credit card companies unilaterally change the terms of their agreement with consumers by mailing a notice of the changes along with the monthly bill. Take the time to read the changes. If you do not like the new terms, cancel the card. Using the card after changes go into effect is construed as your acceptance of them.

As a point of interest, merchants do not have the right to require you to make a minimum purchase in order to use your credit card. According to The Better Business Bureau, the Visa and MasterCard contracts with merchants expressly forbid such requirements. American Express and Discover do not specifically prohibit minimums. However, both state that merchants cannot charge higher minimums for their cards than for other cards they accept. If a merchant accepts Visa or MasterCard, he or she cannot require a minimum charge for either Discover or American Express.

Following are banks offering low interest-rate Visa and Master-Cards you may want to investigate:

- Chevy Chase Federal Savings Bank. 800-777-9901 (11.9 percent, no annual fee for the first year, and 1 percent cash back on all purchases over $1,000).
- AFBA Industrial Bank. 800-776-2265 (12.5 percent variable interest rate, no annual fee, and a 25-day grace period).
- Consumer National Bankcard. 800-862-1616 (9.9 percent variable interest rate, no annual fee, and a 25-day grace period).
- *Penny Pinching* authors Lee and Barbara Simmons recommend the Discover Card to people who *always* pay the charged àmount in full each month (Discover has a high interest rate). But, Discover charges no fee, gives users a 1-percent discount, and has a 25-day grace period from the time of billing until the payment is due.

If you still want to consider more credit cards than listed here, Bankcard Holders of America is a nonprofit organization funded solely by membership dues ($18 per year). Members receive a bimonthly newsletter about credit and personal finance issues, as well as educational pamphlets on credit-related topics. Their money-saving lists are:

- "No Annual Fee List" including banks that offer credit cards without charging a fee.
- "Fair Deal List" of cards offering low interest rates.
- "Secured Card List" of banks that issue cards to consumers with no credit or a poor credit history if they are willing to put up a security fee.

They will send the lists to non-members for a very small fee. They are located at 460 Spring Park Place, Suite 1000, Herndon, VA 22070, 703-481-1110.

Anyone who has ever had a credit card, I venture to say, has had a fight with the credit card company about a bill at one time or another. Frustrating is too much of an understatement to describe getting an error corrected. Knowing some basic facts about your rights (protected by the Federal Fair Credit Billing Act) may make the process less time-consuming.

1. Notify the creditor in writing of the mistake. Your letter should include your name and address, the account number, and a copy of the incorrect bill (and copies of any receipts or canceled checks that supports your position). An inspirational closing for the letter is, "I expect to hear from you about this matter within 30 days, as provided by law."
2. Your letter must be acknowledged within 30 days.
3. Resolution must come within two billing periods or 90 days, whichever comes first. If the credit company fails to meet its obligations under the time limit, it may not be able to collect the full amount owed, even when you're the one in error.

If you continue to disagree and refuse to pay, the credit company can report you delinquent to the credit bureau, restrict your credit and institute collection proceedings. However, it must inform the credit bureau that the amount is under dispute. It must also report to you the name and address of any credit bureaus or reporting agency that it contacts.

Two credit tidbits you may not know about: If you receive a solicitation saying that you have "pre-approved" credit, and you accept, the bank must grant you the credit, according to a little-publicized regulation of the Federal Trade Commission, to wit: 16 C.F. R., section 604 (3)(A)(6). Banks and credit card companies may not use that phrase as an enticement; if they use it, they grant it.

"Right of offset" is a phrase to avoid in any bank loan agreement. This gives the bank the right to remove "late" loan payments from your savings and checking accounts with them.

5. Credit bureaus and what they know about you

Regional credit bureaus collect and distribute the information retail and credit card companies report to them. They do not check the accuracy of it. You may not recognize the person profiled in a credit report bearing your name.

Of the nation's 1,200 credit bureaus, the five major companies are:

TRW Credit Data	Trans Union Credit Informa-
Chilton Corp.	tion Company
CBI-The Credit Bureau Inc.	CSC Credit Services Inc.

Another bureau maintaining personal information is the Medical Information Bureau (MIB). There is no charge to see if MIB has a file on you, or to correct it if there is an error. You can write to MIB at P.O. Box 105, Essex Station, Boston, MA 02112. The phone number is 617-426-3660.

How's your credit rating? Do you pay your bills on time? Credit reporting is a tricky proposition at best. Doing all the right things doesn't *necessarily* give you a good rating. Here are suggestions on how to clean up, and then protect your credit rating.

1. Obtain a copy of your credit report. Send a written request to the credit bureau and pay a nominal fee, or apply for credit and get refused. Then you're entitled to a free copy if you request it in writing within 30 days of the credit refusal.

TRW will send you one free copy a year if you send a written request to its National Consumer Relations Center, P.O. Box 2350, Chatsworth, CA 91313-2350. You will need to include the following personal information in your letter: proof of your present address (photocopy of a driver's license, current utility bill or current credit card bill), Social Security number, date of birth, spouse's name, your address for the past five years with zip codes. Since these identification requirements can change easily, it would be wise to check with a TRW office in your area before mailing your request.

2. Read the report carefully, noting any items you feel are wrong, questionable, out-of-date or not yours. Make sure all the information is up-to-date, including your name and address. Check your employer's name, address, telephone number. Check your "employed since" date, previous address, and your own telephone number. If you are self-employed, it should show that as well.

3. Correct the report. Use a red pen to draw a rectangle around each erroneous item. Highlight the same item again in yellow. Number the items you are disputing (1, 2, 3, 4). Do not dispute more than four items per letter. You may send a second letter in one week disputing another four items.

To avoid being mistaken for a credit repair company, do not type your cover letter—print it by hand. A legitimate "credit repair" company cannot do anything for consumers that the consumers cannot do for themselves. A number of credit repair companies advertise on matchbook covers and charge steep prices to produce few, if any, results. One of their techniques is to send typed form letters to the credit bureaus on behalf of their "clients." This is why you must print your letter by hand.

List the disputed items, giving the number shown on the report (1, 2, 3, 4), the company name, the subscriber number and briefly explaining why the item is not correct. Make sure you print legibly.

4. Send by certified mail, receipt requested, your letter and a copy of the report showing the disputed items. Be sure to make a copy of the entire package with your registered mail receipt attached. You should expect a response within three to six weeks.

5. If you do not receive a response by the sixth week *exactly*, make another copy of the package and send it again. Mark on envelope: 2ND REQUEST PLEASE RESPOND IMMEDIATELY.

6. Check the results of your dispute by comparing the copy with the highlights when you receive the credit bureau response. Some items may have stayed the same. Dispute them again. After several tries the items will be corrected.

The credit bureau is compelled by law to conduct an investigation of the items you claim are in error and, under the law, to correct them if your claim is true.

If you are refused credit, you have the right to know the *specific reasons* why your credit was refused. The legislation that commands this compliance are the Federal Credit Reporting Act (FCRA) and the Equal Credit Opportunity Act (ECOA).

This seems like a lot of work, and you may be thinking that it would be advantageous to join a membership service that promises to keep you posted about changes in your credit report. TRW has a membership service that is supposed to help you keep the information accurate on your credit profile. Basically, the membership benefits are that you receive a copy of your TRW credit report; you are notified when anyone requests your credit report; you can change your financial profile, and you can register credit cards.

I did a three-month trial membership since the charge was reasonable and I thought it would be easier to get some items corrected. It took a month to receive my membership materials and credit report. The first thing I noticed was that my report was suspiciously short—there were no records on me. My first use of the new membership was to correct the spelling of my name on their records.

Here is humorist Dave Barry description of TRW Credentials:

> *TRW is a large company that collects credit information about people and sells it. According to the TRW Credentials [advertisement] offer, if I give them $20 a year, they'll let me see my information. In other words—correct me if I am wrong here—they're telling me that I should give them $20 a year so I can look at the information ABOUT ME that they collected WITHOUT MY PERMISSION and have been selling for years to GOD ALONE KNOWS WHO so I can see if it's INCORRECT.*

Here is Ralph Nader's recommendation for reporting agency membership clubs: *"DON'T BUY."*

6. When you have credit problems

If you need help with paying your debts, consider seeking the assistance of a Consumer Credit Counseling Service (CCCS). This is a nonprofit organization with more than 200 offices located in 44 states. CCCS counselors will try to arrange a repayment plan that is acceptable to you and your creditors. They will also help you set up a realistic budget and plan future expenses. These services are offered at little or no charge to you.

To locate the nearest CCCS office, contact: National Foundation for Consumer Credit, Inc., 8701 Georgia Avenue, Suite 507, Silver Spring, MD 20910, 800-388-CCCS.

I used the Budget and Credit Counseling Services (BuCCS), which is a nonprofit agency licensed by the New York State Banking Department, to assist me in paying off employee loans when I was involved in the lawsuit with my former company. If you receive help from one of these agencies, creditors may report your accounts as being paid slowly, or that you have entered a debt adjustment program. If creditors have turned your account over to collection agencies that hound you, the service will remind them of the laws that protect consumers against harassment, such as the Federal Fair Debt Collection Practices Act.

There are a couple of points under the Act that consumers are not always aware of.

1. If the consumer writes a letter to the collection agency or attorney instructing them to cease further contact, they must. The attorney or agency may write to acknowledge that there will be no further contact, or to inform of action they will take, *not threaten to take.*

2. Collectors are prohibited from putting any information on the outside of envelopes other than a return address. Their name may appear on the envelope if it does not indicate the letter is about debt collection.

7. Protect yourself against fraud

Did you know that there are career con artists who specialize in "dumpster diving?" They make their livings searching trash for credit card receipts, canceled checks and old deposit slips in order to fraudulently use other people's credit. Whereas we all take a few precautions to prevent an unauthorized use of our cards, destroying transaction carbons and such, here are three more ways you may not know about.

1. After using an ATM, always take your receipts and transaction records with you.

2. If you are paying for merchandise by check, don't let the clerk write your credit card number on it. This practice is now illegal in many states.

3. Before you toss unwanted promotional mailings from your bank or credit card company, check to see if your account or other identification is on the material.

8. What to do when *you're* the creditor

Particularly if you're working as a freelance temp, consultant or managing your own business startup, you will learn that, unfortunately, not all clients pay in 30 days. Some corporations pay on a 120-day schedule. Some do not pay at all. This plays havoc with the cash flow. It makes sense to give some thought to a credit and collection policy for your business, to put it in writing for yourself and perhaps for your clients as well. If, for example, you plan to charge for an initial appointment, be sure the potential client understands this.

What kind of client information will help you assess if you will be paid in a timely fashion for your services? Consider gathering some or all of the following information from potential clients. You can devise some type of "work order" form for them to complete, or you can informally ask them in preliminary conversations.

- Information about their business: Is it a partnership, sole proprietorship or corporation. How long have they been in business? What is their bank name and address? Obtain the names of three businesses or vendors they are doing business with to check bill-paying history.

- Information about the individual client: Get a complete name, address, home phone number, spouse name, driver's license and Social Security number. Include, if you care to, employment information for both client and spouse (name, address, length of time, telephone). It never hurts to get the name of their bank and personal references.

As always, please give some thought beforehand to how you will handle it if the customer doesn't give complete information or if the credit history is poor.

To come up with a credit policy for your services, take into consideration the following points:

1. How much work will you complete before payment must be made? How do you want to be paid? Cash? Check? Credit card? Money order?
2. What about discounts and fees? Will you offer discounts for prompt payment? Will you attach service charges for late payments or bounced checks? Under what conditions will you expect advance payment?
3. What is your return policy? To what extent will you "guarantee satisfaction"?
4. If the client wishes to terminate the amount of agreed-upon services, how much notice will you require? Will you charge penalties?

Before beginning any work for a client:

1. Communicate your credit and collection policies as it pertains to the work you will do for them.
2. Get a signed contract (or letter of agreement, order form, purchase order).
3. Get a deposit, if possible.

Invoices for your services do not need to be complicated. Basically, you want to keep track of clients, dates and amounts.

On the following page is a simple system that works for me.

DTA automation consulting

Mr. Kevin Downs
Warren and Associates, Inc.
345 Park Avenue South
New York, NY 10016

For professional services:

April 26-30, 1993
33 hours @ $23.50 per hour $775.50

Please make check payable to Diane L. Thrailkill
Tax I.D. 13-2345618

Invoice number: WA-9312
Invoice date: April 30, 1993

1234 Autumn Road, White Plains, NY 10001
(914) 555-4321

The invoice number tells me the following information: "WA" stands for the initials of the client (Warren & Associates). The number "9312" gives me the year (1993) and the number of invoices (12) for that company in that year.

Along with invoices services rendered comes the collections of unpaid amounts sometimes. Suppose, in spite of your clearly stated, written policy, the client doesn't pay as expected. You need to have a plan of action on how to proceed. Give some thought to these suggestions:

1. When will you present/send an invoice? What will be the interval between statements? What will the message be on follow-up invoices? How many will you send before telephoning?

2. What will you say when you call?

3. Under what conditions will you take small payments on account? Turn over to a collection agency? Go to Small Claims Court? Write it off?

One of my former agencies stiffed me for some training services. I telephoned them several times when I didn't receive the check. (How many times can the check be lost in the mail?) I went to the agency three times to pick up the check, only to have yet another screw-up keep it from being ready. I finally caught on.

I wrote to the president of the agency and sent it certified mail, receipt requested. The letter outlined the sequence of events leading up to my letter. In the closing paragraph I said, "If you were unaware of this situation, perhaps you'd like to rectify it in some way. If you *did* know about it, and this is normal business practice for your agency, please be advised I will be delighted to share the story with other agencies, clients and temps."

The president called the same day he received the letter. I had a check the next day.

If you don't get a response from those clients who owe you money, you may be forced to take the matter to Small Claims Court. The cost to file and serve papers is usually less than $50, there is no need for a lawyer, the procedure and language are designed for lay people, not much time is involved (usually 30 to 60 days), you can address problems where high dollar amounts are involved, and there is judgment by default if the defendant doesn't show up in court.

There are procedural variations within the many counties of 50 states. To get the precise information about how it works in your locality go to the Small Claims Court office of your county courthouse and request information.

I have given you a lot to think about, especially when it comes to getting paid for your services. One of the things I do in my computer consulting capacity is to train workers how to restore erased files and retrieve "lost" data. I know, at some point, they are going to inadvertently erase important information. I also know, having taken them through the steps of what to do, they will restore their data, more or less calmly, without too much difficulty.

The same concept applies here. Better to take steps ahead of time to *prevent* problems, rather than to later spend considerable energy trying to *solve* them. The best time to learn how to handle a crisis is when you're not in the middle of it.

Further reading

The Check Is Not In The Mail, Leonard Sklar, Baroque Publishing, 1990.

Penny Pinching, Lee and Barbara Simmons, Bantam, 1993.

The Frugal Shopper, Ralph Nader and Wesley J. Smith, Center for Study of Responsive Law, 1992.

If Time Is Money, No Wonder I'm Not Rich, Mary L. Sprouse, Simon & Schuster, 1993.

Your Rights as a Consumer, Legal Tips for Savvy Purchasing of Goods, Services and Credit, 2nd ed., Marc R. Lieberman, Career Press, 1994.

Solving Your Financial Problems, 2nd ed., Richard L. Strohm, Career Press, 1994.

Life After Debt, Bob Hammond, Career Press, 1994.

Barrons (a weekly financial newspaper) and *Money* magazine (monthly) both list credit cards with the current lowest annual percentage rates in each issue.

Consumer publications

Another resource for low-cost publications on any number of consumer-interest topics is your local Department of Consumer Affairs. Examples of pertinent titles in New York City are "Ranking Banking: The Consumer Score Card," and "Credit Card Interest Rates." You can request a publications list by writing to them 42 Broadway, New York, NY 10004, or calling 212-487-4278.

Chapter 10

Laws, Insurance, Taxes

....

Any number of laws regulate temporary employees and self-employed people. Having a nodding acquaintance with a few of them allows you to fully exercise more of the available options, and helps avoid the gathering of information the usual way—one mistake at a time.

In all instances the information in this chapter is furnished as a guide, to alert readers to the ramifications of various actions, and to furnish resources for seeking professional assistance and more detailed information. *In no way is it to be construed as expert advice.*

Unemployment insurance

Temping and collecting benefits: Agencies, as temporary employment companies, pay into the state unemployment insurance fund. Temps, as agency employees, can collect unemployment insurance, provided they qualify under the laws of their state. For instance, to qualify in New York, typically you would have to work at least 20 weeks a year and have at least $1,600 in covered earnings. A week of employment means a Monday-through-Sunday week in which you had *some* covered work, even as little as a day or part of a day.

This is a general example. The eligibility rules are quite specific and, of course, differ from state to state. To determine what your benefits are, request a booklet of claimant unemployment information from your state department for unemployment insurance.

You can work as a temporary employee while collecting unemployment benefits, provided the benefit and temp salary together do not add up to more than the gross of the amount of your weekly benefit. For instance, if your benefit is $280 weekly, and your temp income for one week is that amount or more, you will not receive a stipend for that period. On the other hand, if your temp income is $150, you would receive a $130 stipend to bring the total back to $280.

The earned portion of the benefit is not lost by working; it is extended. However, it is not extended beyond the 52 consecutive weeks of the benefit year, and you may drown in the paperwork needing completion to collect a stipend.

The agency also must fill out unemployment forms on temps who work for them and collect a stipend. Unscrupulous agencies have been known to offer work to those temps at a considerably lower hourly rate, with the veiled threat to report them to the unemployment agency if the work was refused. Here are two suggestions to keep this from happening:

- Discuss with both the agency counselor and the unemployment person the mechanics of temping and collecting unemployment. Get specific examples of what constitutes a "refusal of work."
- Reach an agreement with the agency on some ground rules, such as the lowest rate they will offer and you will accept, appropriate and inappropriate assignments; accepting or refusing work out of your field.

Worker's compensation/state disability insurance

Worker's compensation covers employees for work-related injuries and illnesses, paying such expenses as medical bills and a percentage of lost wages. In more extreme cases, it pays for funeral expenses, survivor's benefits and provides liability against the employer for an injury, illness or death. The specific illnesses or accidents a worker may be compensated for are regulated at the state level and may differ from state to state. In general, most states cover easily identified work-related injuries, such as back injuries related to heavy lifting.

Temporary employment agencies pay into these funds. Temps, as employees of these agencies, are covered, as provided under the laws of their states.

"It's a state law"

All states have laws on the books to protect workers from various adverse or hazardous working conditions. These laws are supposed to benefit the workers. Don't blindly accept at face value that you must agree to certain restrictions or conditions because it is touted as a state law. Educate yourself as to what the alleged "law" is, then use it to your advantage.

An example I use in my seminars is the mandated lunch hour. Some states require businesses to provide employees with a half-hour uninterrupted lunch time. Employees are not paid for this time. The purpose is to provide a work-free period for employees to eat lunch in peace, should they wish to. When client companies have rules requiring temps or employees to take a daily lunch break between the hours of noon and 2 p.m., it is a company rule, not a state law. Work for the company—or not, as you wish. I prefer to work through lunch. Most days, I take my alleged "mandatory" lunch hour after 5 p.m.

Exemptions and taxes

Full-time temporary employment. Agencies withhold taxes and FICA according to the number of exemptions listed on your W-2 form. However, when you work for multiple agencies, you may work for one or two days for several of them during a week. The agencies may not withhold taxes on one day's pay. If you prefer to utilize withholding to receive a tax refund, you may be surprised, instead, with a tax bill for April 15. Be aware that this happens and talk to your agencies about your preferences.

Part-time temping with other business interests. You still file a W-2 form with the agency. If you have other business interests and pay quarterly taxes as I do, you might want to consider claiming the maximum number of exemptions or listing yourself as exempt (only FICA will be deducted). Talk to your tax professional to determine what would be best for your situation.

Some temporary employment agencies will pay temps as independent contractors, withholding no taxes or FICA and filing a 1099 at the end of the year if the wages exceed $600. You, in turn, file the 1099 forms with your tax return for income over $600 for which no tax was deducted.

Self-employment has certain tax advantages. To maximize the number of deductions available to you as a person engaged in a variety of money-earning activities, you might want to discuss with your tax professional the merits of the following as they apply to you:

1. Obtaining a DBA (doing business as) certificate

2. Obtaining a separate tax ID

3. Paying quarterly estimated taxes

Estimated quarterly taxes are due four times a year: January 15, April 15, June 15 and September 15. Tax IDs are obtained by completing and filing Form SS-4 Application for Employer Identification Number.

Qualifying the home office

Prior to writing this segment, I called my tax professional to ask if the requirements had changed for the 1993/1994 tax season. She had not received any recent communication about it but suggested I call the IRS directly. "If the language has changed," she said, "the IRS will send you a current pamphlet. If you are told there are no changes in the law, call back two additional times to verify that there are no changes. That's what I do. The have to give me the same information three times before I believe it."

A word to the wise: Getting through to the IRS takes persistence, the lines are often busy. Avoid calling at lunchtime or on Mondays. Those are especially busy times.

The IRS qualifies a home office as space that is used "...exclusively and regularly for activities to a trade or business, and be either: 1) the principal place of business; 2) a place to meet and deal with patients, clients or customers; or 3) located in a separate, free-standing structure."

If the taxpayer works as someone else's employee and *is not* self-employed, the home office must be: 1) a condition of employment; and 2) for the employer's convenience, not the employee's.

Indirect expenses such as utilities, real estate taxes and depreciation are permitted on a percentage basis. the net square footage calculation determining the percent of those business/personal areas from the total square footage. The business cannot show a loss. You must show a net profit, no matter how small. It cannot be a hobby or a passive activity such as managing investments.

A percentage deduction is used for a home office:

- Rent or mortgage.
- Homeowner's/renter's insurance.
- Utilities: gas, electricity, water, heat.
- Real-estate taxes, school taxes.
- Depreciation on office portion.
- Telephone.

Independent contractor

In recent articles about the perils of temporary employment, one of the facts cited is that workers are paid as independent contractors. What does this mean? How are these independent contractors different from permanent employees?

Employers have a number of obligations to regular employees that they do not have to independent contractors (freelancers, consultants). For permanent employees they pay into those funds that provide worker's compensation, unemployment insurance, state disability benefits; they withhold employment taxes from paychecks. Independent contractors are paid on a 1099 Form, no deductions are taken out.

The IRS considers independent contractors as those who operate under written or oral agreements that define work to be performed by a given date for an hourly or fixed amount from which no taxes are deducted. Independent contractors pay quarterly taxes. The IRS has 20 "qualifying rules" to distinguish these independent business people who offer services to multiple clients from employees. Questionable cases are decided on an individual basis by performance in the following categories:

1. **Instructions.** Independent contractors work without being told when, where or how to do the task.
2. **Training.** Independent contractors come into the job with skills in place. They would not receive training from client.
3. **Integration.** Independent contractors are not a part of daily routine; business can operate without a contractor's services.
4. **Performance.** Independent contractors may assign others to do work.
5. **Cost of goods/assistants.** Independent contractors hire, train, supervise and pay assistants; they pay for materials as part of contract.
6. **Work relationship.** Independent contractors have a different relationship than the employee who performs work frequently at recurring intervals as part of an ongoing relationship with company.
7. **Schedule.** Independent contractors set their own schedules and hours.
8. **Hours worked.** Independent contractors are available to work for multiple companies rather than one only.
9. **Work location.** Independent contractors are not restricted to working on company premises.
10. **Work sequence.** Independent contractors do their work in whatever sequence they determine.
11. **Accountability.** Independent contractors are not accountable to the client for daily activities.
12. **Payment method.** Independent contractors are usually paid by the job or on straight commission rather than hourly, weekly, monthly or annually.

    (This certainly isn't true in New York City. Most consultants are paid by the hour.)

13. **Expenses.** Independent contractors pay their own business and travel expenses (but bill company for them when part of a project).

14. **Tools.** Independent contractors supply their own tools or equipment.

15. **Investment.** Independent contractors put a significant investment in equipment or facilities in order to perform their services.

16. **Profit or loss.** Independent contractors do not receive a salary. They either make a profit or suffer a loss.

17. **Number of business customers.** Independent contractors may work for multiple companies at any one time.

18. **Availability.** Independent contractors are available to work for multiple companies.

19. **Termination.** Independent contractors must be paid if they produce the results specified in contract. Employees can be fired.

20. **Right to quit.** Independent contractors are legally obligated to meet contract terms, which can include a clause to end the work relationship.

Business records: How long do you keep them?

The general rule is that receipts may be discarded three years from the date of tax return is filed or two years after the tax is paid, whichever is later. For example, your 1993 taxes will be due April 15, 1994. The records should be kept until April, 1997. The IRS has six years to get you if you under-report your gross income by more than 25 percent. If you file a fraudulent return, or don't file one at all, there is no time limit in prosecuting you.

Some personal records are forever (or until you sell the item):

- Expensive insured items such as jewelry, furs, art, etc.
- Investments.
- Property records.

- Home improvement.
- Escrow or settlement statements.
- Refinancing.

Self-employed business records:

6 years: Accounts payable/accounts receivable ledgers.
Expired contracts.
Employee time reports.
Disability and sick benefit records.
Former employee records.
W-4 forms (withholding statements).
Freight bills.

8 years: Payroll records, including canceled payroll checks, time reports and earning records.

Forever: Tax returns (Form 4506 is "Request for Copy of Tax Form," should you wish a missing copy).
Depreciable assets (for three years after you sell) such as computer, office equipment.
IRA records (for three years after funds are withdrawn).

Organizing business expense categories

Your tax reporting will be facilitated if you categorize and separate your expense receipts. At the end of the year, it takes a minimum of time to total each category and prepare summary expense sheets for the tax preparer.

I find my taxed income falls into three categories: "salaried" temp income on which FICA is paid by me and the agency, consulting income and writing/teaching income. I break my expense categories into three segments: consultant, writer/teacher, temp/private citizen. I use a numerical accordion file that has 31 compartments to categorize the expenses. I put labels with the expense categories written on them over the numbered partitions in alphabetical order (more or less). My breakdown is shown on the next two pages.

Writing/Seminars
Books/periodicals
Editor/Agent
Equipment
Education

Postage
Professional memberships/Union
Stationery/office supplies
Travel

Temporary Employment
FICA
Income

IRA
Medicare/Disability

DTA Automation
Auto: lease, insurance
Bank fees, checks
Bank loan
Books/periodicals
Condo insurance
Charity (receipts)
Doctors
Education
Equipment
Interest income
KEOGH
Medical Insurance
Memberships

Mortgage interest
Over-the-counter medicine
Postage
Prescriptions
Safe deposit box
School taxes
Stationery/office supplies
Tax preparation
Town taxes
Travel
Utilities: electricity, heat,
   telephone, water

At the end of the year, I total the receipts in each category and give the summary sheets to my tax preparer. She takes the appropriate percentages for deductions and depreciation and completes the myriad forms for all of it.

Common deductions for freelancers

Bank account/checks/fees
Interest paid on business loans
Business travel
Education
Transportation
Membership dues

Work-related periodicals,
   newspapers
State sales tax
Safe deposit box
Moving expenses (more than
   35 miles)

IRA/KEOGH
Subcontracting
Uniforms
Tools, supplies
General office supplies
Stationery, business cards,
  postage
Answering service/machine
Office equipment
Bad debts (costs incurred)

Gifts and holiday cards
Legal services
Financial planning services
Entertainment
Insurance
Repair services
Equipment/furniture rental
Printing/copying services
Cleaning services and/or supplies
Advertising, public relations

Remember everyone is different. Run the deductions by a tax professional for a careful check, or consult with the IRS if you are particularly self-abusive.

Red flags

Each year the IRS selects a random number of tax returns for a thorough scrutiny under the Taxpayer Compliance Measurement program that analyzes all items on tax returns. Most audits result from a screening of tax returns by the "discriminant function system" computer program that assigns scores according to a secret mathematical formula. However, tax experts say that some of the red flags are:

1. Not listing all sources of income.

2. Large deductions for casualty losses.

3. Large contributions to charity.

4. High percent formula used to compute deductions for rental property or home business.

5. Deductions that are high relative to income. Meticulous documentation should be kept if you have deductions in the following areas:
    - Barter
    - Home Office
    - Business Travel
    - Calculating percentages for business entertainment

153

Finding professional assistance

Tax Preparer? Bookkeeper? Accountant? Which professional do you need? That is dependent on the complexity of your business activities. The CPA Communications Council and the American Institute of Certified Public Accountants offers the following questions to aid your decision.

1. Do you need help with personal financial problems, income tax returns, retirement planning or estate planning?
2. Will your business require help in putting together its financial statements?
3. Will your financial statements require an audit or a review?
4. Which of the following services does your business require—accounting, auditing, tax advice or consulting?
5. Will you need help preparing a business loan application?
6. Will you need help preparing special reports to government agencies?

Shopping for the right tax professional

Speak with people in the same field as you are and, if possible, engaged in similar activities. Ask other small business owners, the chamber of commerce or small business council in your community for referrals.

1. Before you talk with the professional, have some idea of your plans and objectives. Make a list of questions. Compile information about business or personal financial decisions under consideration so you can ask specific questions.
2. Make sure the person is licensed to practice in your state.
3. Talk frankly about fees. They will depend on the type of services you require, the prevailing costs in the community and the complexity of your work.

The owner of my neighborhood dry cleaners referred me to my tax person about 15 years ago. She services numerous small businesses in Westchester County. Her business started in her basement/family room about 20 years ago and grew to be the sole support of her family.

She is still based at home, but has had an "above-the-ground" office for the last 10 years. Her fees are still reasonable.

Contracts and letters of agreement

It is always best to put your agreement in writing. Think of it as a professional approach to defining what each party is responsible for. Write up what was agreed to by telephone: the quantities, money, time frame, delivery date and payment terms. Sign it, send it by fax or mail to the other party for a signature. It doesn't have to be a complicated form to stand up in court. Usually a letter to the client spelling out the points of the agreement between you is sufficient. It is always a good idea to include a description of the work you have agreed to do, the date it should be completed, the location where the work will be performed, the amount, and method and timing of payment for work.

Contracts can be oral or written. Whether or not an oral contract is enforceable is a legal question. If something is important to you, get it in writing.

When to consult an attorney

In some cases, it is better to spend a little money for legal consultation first, before you sign the contract or write the letter of agreement, than to spend lots of money afterwards to extricate yourself from a bad situation. Consult an attorney if:

- Significant amounts of money are involved, for work performed over a lengthy period of time.
- The terms of a contract are confusing or difficult to understand.
- You are writing or signing a partnership agreement.
- You are protecting an invention.
- You are buying a business or a franchise.

Shopping for an attorney

The time to shop for an attorney is when you don't need one. Ask friends, colleagues, or small business owners for referrals. If you use the local bar association referral service, heed the following:

Temp By Choice

In his book *Kill All the Lawyers,* Sloan Bashinsky, Esq., states that most referral services do not check out the credentials of participating lawyers. He claims lawyers who accept referrals from them are either new or are not busy enough. He further counsels to avoid:

- Lawyers with conflicts of interest.
- Friends.
- Relatives.
- "Practicing" lawyers (They don't serve an internship or do a residency under the supervision of other lawyers. All they need is a law license to "practice" on you.)
- Those who aren't busy.
- Those who are too busy.
- Stone-age-with-no-computer.
- Those with personal problems such as divorce, custody battles, substance abuse and illness.

Try to chat with the attorney first by telephone, then set up an appointment to interview. There should either be no charge or a minimal charge for this first encounter. It is a get-acquainted meeting, one hour or less, where you will not be asking for legal advice. Remember you are the *employer*, the attorney is the potential *employee*.

Questions to ask

1. What is her/his specialty? How many matters does she/he handle a year that are similar to your situation? You are after frequency, not generalities or one success story.
2. Who in the firm will handle your business? If it is another lawyer or a paralegal, you should have a similar meeting (at another time) with that person.
3. How large are the businesses usually served?
4. Ask about continuing education. One way to judge competence is by the amount of time the lawyer has devoted to keeping up with changes in the law through continuing legal education.

5. Ask for the names of a few clients for whom she/he has done similar work. If the attorney is any good, several clients will be willing to talk to you.

Nonverbal clues

Office: Is the decor somewhat tasteful? Lavish? Run-down? Is it neat? Disorganized and messy? Is there a computer? Law library?

Lawyer: Is she/he polite? Does she/he look you in the eye when speaking? Is she/he having telephone calls held? If not, the individual is not concentrating on you. Is she/he a good listener? Does she/he dress neatly? A disorganized, messy person in a similar office will keep your matters or case that way as well. Do the two of you seem to be compatible? If you feel uncomfortable about the lawyer in any of these areas, it's not a good sign.

Attorney fees and expenses

Fees are based not only on the time and labor. Especially in legal actions, they are based on the novelty and difficulty of the questions raised, and the skill needed to perform the required legal services. The attorney also factors in whether the acceptance of a case will preclude other employment, time limitations imposed, amount of damages sought and the fee customarily charged in the locality for similar legal services.

Attorneys are entitled to reimbursement for expenses incurred in connection with your work—travel costs, meals away from the office, telephone calls, postage, etc. When they are discussing or working on your matter, the meter runs, always.

Get a firm understanding about costs:

* How much per hour?
* How many hours should the work take? (You won't get a precise answer for this one.)
* How will you be expected to pay? Lump sum or in installments?
* Ask what you can do to trim costs.

Keeping it professional

If you have anything important to tell your lawyer, do it in writing. Lawyers often forget to write down what you tell them, it's the only way you can prove what you told your attorney if a problem develops between the two of you.

Follow up after a meeting or telephone conversation with a recap of the topics discussed and what the decisions were.

Request copies of all letters and documents prepared on your behalf.

Don't sign any document or paper until you understand the full import of what you are signing.

Money savers

- Prepare a check list before each visit or telephone call. Keep an accurate track of time. If there is any discrepancy in billing between your time log and the attorney's, call attention to it immediately.

- Provide the attorney with copies of all pertinent material, including your notes about it.

- Put your facts in chronological order, using full names of the people involved and attach all relevant documents.

- Use "briefing papers" to describe complicated background material or incidents. This way you are not paying the attorney to "interview" you and take notes.

- Use boilerplate contracts or forms whenever you can. Most libraries have books with industry-specific standard forms that include explanations and suggestions on use.

- Read up on any routine matters to ascertain if there are preliminary tasks you can do prior to a consultation—filing of papers, trade name or trademark search, etc.

- Do some of the tasks yourself: photocopying, delivering papers, etc.

- Have your lawyer write out the precise legal questions when research is needed. Get your local law school placement office to recommend a student to pore over records. You'll pay a fraction of what a law firm will charge to have the work done by a junior associate. Obviously, your lawyer reviews the student's research and directs further inquiry if it is needed.

- Gather exhibits yourself instead of having the lawyer's clerk put them together.

Unemployment insurance, worker's compensation, independent contractors, taxes, attorneys—tedious topics all. This potpourri chapter has given you highlights of information in these areas as well as where to seek further guidance to conduct your business dealings. All this within the framework of regulation designed to benefit you. A small investment in knowledge, thoughtfully administered, will generate sizable dividends.

Consumer group

HALT is an organization committed to improving the quality, reducing the cost and increasing the accessibility of the civil justice system. It publishes a number of manuals and books to assist consumers' handling of their own legal affairs and to become informed users of legal services. It also provides attorney referrals to people who are bringing charges against attorneys.

You can contact this organization by writing to or calling: HALT: An Organization For Legal Reform, 1319 F Street NW, Suite 300, Washington, D.C. 20004, 202-347-9600.

Further reading

Kill All the Lawyers, Sloan Bashinsky, Esq., Prentice Hall, 1986.

You Don't Always Need a Lawyer, Craig Kubey, et. al., Consumer Reports Books, 1991.

Using a Lawyer...and What to Do if Things Go Wrong, Kay Ostberg in association with HALT, Random House, 1990.

NOLO Press is the largest publisher of self-help law books. Call for a catalog of listings, 800-992-NOLO. Residents of California, call 800-445-NOLO.

Chapter 11

Benefits:
Medical, Disability,
Pensions

Ask anyone what is the biggest drawback to temporary employment, and I am willing to bet the answer will be "lack of benefits." The purpose of this chapter is to provide information about the legislation and options that already exist, no matter how limited, and to suggest a few avenues of exploration for better options.

Currently, the pension and health care legislation on the books offers minimal protection to both temporary workers and leased workers. In addition, it continues to amaze me that the majority of temps that I have come in contact with seem unaware that they are covered under state laws for unemployment, disability and worker's compensation. The agencies are failing to educate their employees about basic benefits.

There is no such thing as a free lunch. While permanent employees may have numerous "benefits," there are several tradeoffs. The lack of personal freedom and minimal flexibility in working hours/days are but two.

At this writing, industry pundits expect federal legislation within the next two years to require agencies to provide health and pension benefits to their temporaries. Until such time as these predictions prove true or false, here are some alternatives.

First, let's take a look at what is already on the books under federal regulations, specifically the Tax Reform Act of 1986 (TRA).

Employee leasing

Employee leasing uses the concept of temporary services within the core work force of a corporation or company. Here's how it works. The corporation will terminate a group of employees, who will then be hired by a third party—the leasing company—and leased back to their original company. The leasing company takes over the day-to-day personnel administration: the hiring, firing, payroll, benefits, worker's compensation and unemployment insurance premiums. Until 1986, this arrangement owed much of its appeal to the "safe harbor" it provided employers from normal pension obligations. Thus, a company could provide generous pension benefits to executives, yet exclude the bulk of its work force, the leased employees.

The Tax Reform Act of 1986 eliminated the tax shelter for top-heavy pension plans. It provides for a number of "tests" to be applied to determine whether a company's health insurance and pension plans are nondiscriminatory. It prohibits a company from excluding leased employees from pension plans if they comprise more than 20 percent of its work force. It raises the employer (leasing company) contributions to employees' pension fund from 7.5 to 10 percent.

In addition, emerging case law supports the view that the typical staff leasing arrangement establishes a co-employer relationship between the leasing service and the client company. This joint-employer arrangement includes joint liabilities for discriminatory hiring and other violations of labor laws, which tends to make it less attractive to companies. A further disincentive is that a company relinquishes the day-to-day control of its leased employees to the third-party leasing company in exchange for the administrative services it provides.

Apparently, the employee leasing business needs a modest capital outlay to start up. It has attracted its share of underfunded operators who fail and leave behind unfunded pension benefits, unpaid taxes and bounced paychecks.

Employees of temporary employment companies

Section 414(n) of the Tax Reform Act applies to temps. Temp agencies must include their temp employees in the "tests" of their own pension and health insurance plans. However, the exclusions exempt a sizable chunk of temps from any coverage. Excluded are employees:

- of less than six months (for health insurance)
- of less than one year (for pension plans)
- under the age of 21
- who work less than 17½ hours weekly
- who are covered under a collective bargaining agreement

If temps perform "substantial services" (1,500 hours in a year, or approximately six months) to a company and comprise more than 5 percent of its total "lower-paid" work force, the company may have to provide the same health and pension benefits as for their other employees, *or pay taxes on their plan contributions*. The plan benefits to their employees will be counted as taxable income.

When temps are unaware of their rights under the law, they can fall prey to unscrupulous agencies that, in collusion with companies, place them in long-term assignments, "end" the assignment just before the 1,500 hours are reached, then rehire the same temps for a continuation of the same assignment. A variation is where the company next hires the temps as "contract workers" without benefits.

Continuation insurance (COBRA)

The Consolidated Omnibus Budget Reconciliation Act (COBRA) allows persons who currently have group plans through a spouse's employers to continue the coverage after divorce, death, retirement or the event of unemployment or reduced hours of work. Spouses and children can pay premiums and continue the plan for three years. Unemployed workers can continue for 18 months. Employers can charge an administrative fee of up to 4 percent. At the end of the three-year or 18-month period, there is the option of continuing as an individual. However, it won't be at the group rate or at the same level of coverage. The benefit here is that a worker doesn't have to go through insurability requirements or be subjected to pre-existing condition restrictions.

Companies with fewer than 20 employees, or ones with a government, church or self-insured plan are exempt from this law. However, some states have continuation laws that are similar to the federal one. Check with an insurance broker or with the state insurance department for information on a particular company. For questions about COBRA, write to Pension and Welfare Benefits Administration, Division of Technical Assistance and Inquiries, 200 Constitution Ave. NW, Room N5625, Washington, DC 20210.

Finding affordable medical coverage

In addition to federal regulations, a number of state laws address issues of concern to temps. Employees of temporary service companies qualify for these insurance plans as stipulated by the laws of their states.

The National Association of Temporary Services (NATS) sponsors health insurance that can be purchased in segments of 30 to 180 days, covers spouses under 65 and dependent children under 19. This is the most common insurance offered by agencies to its temps. The plan is $250 deductible for each illness or accident, then covers 80 percent for the first $5,000, and 100 percent up to $1 million. It can be renewed one time, for another six months, but any illness claimed is considered "preexisting." NATS also sponsors a long-term medical plan.

The present plans are under revision. The NATS insurance coordinator tells me there may be a new provider insurance company selected as well.

An avenue worthy of investigation is the Health Maintenance Organization (HMO). At this writing, more than 30 million Americans are using over 600 different HMOs in the U.S. Their main attraction is that they provide members with affordable health care, including individual coverage. The most mentioned drawback is that members must use HMO physicians and "approved practices" for that health care. (Have leeches been outlawed, I hope?) Ralph Nader in *The Frugal Shopper,* lists the pluses and minuses:

HMO pluses

- Lower premiums
- No deductibles
- No or minimal ($5) copayments
- Prescriptions paid or minimal copayment ($2 to $5)
- Preventive health care is covered
- Choice of primary care physician (from HMO authorized list)
- Medical records readily available

HMO minuses

- May have to change doctors if you join HMO
- Insufficient testing
- Difficulty in getting: nonplan emergency room treatment, or authorization for treatment outside the plan area, specialists.

Often the state insurance commissioner's office (located in your state capital) has information available to consumers such as a list of HMOs in nearby locations, or insurer complaint ratios (the ratio of unhappy plan members to the total plan membership). The Health Insurance Association of America (HIAA) has a free pamphlet listing all the state commissioner addresses and telephone numbers. Request one by calling 202-223-7808, or write to P.O. Box 41455, Washington, DC 20018.

Co-Op America in conjunction with Alternative Health Insurance Services (AHIS), offers relatively affordable insurance in most states. They can be reached at 1850 "M" Street NW, Suite 700 Washington, DC 20036, 202-872-5307 Insurance questions: 800-331-2713 or 800-966-8467.

Check out membership organizations such as the American Association of University Women (AAUW) or National Writers

Union (NWU). Sometimes a modest membership fee makes it worthwhile to join an association for group medical benefits.

Evaluating health insurance

When looking for medical coverage, use the following questions to gather the information needed to make an informed decision.

1. What is the maximum dollar amount of coverage? If it isn't unlimited, it should be in range of $1 to $2 million.

2. Is the deductible one that you can afford? Is there a carryover at the end of the year? Generally the higher the deductible the lower the premium. For this reason you should take the highest deductible you can afford.

3. Choose a policy with a yearly deductible rather than a per-usage deductible.

4. Are the copayment provisions as least 80 percent/20 percent?

5. Does the policy restore any portion of the maximum benefits once you are well? Some policies will restore all or partial benefits after a period where no claims are submitted.

6. What is the stop-loss amount? This is the expense amount reached after which you stop paying anything toward your medical expense, preventing the 20 percent copayments adding up to an exorbitant amount of money. Some policies pay 100 percent of claims after $5,000, others less.

7. Is the policy noncancelable and guaranteed renewable or conditionally renewable? A conditionally renewable policy means the company would have to cancel all policies and no longer sell health insurance in the state. A good group policy will not necessarily increase its premiums every year. *Ask about the recent premium history.*

8. Are all hospital/doctor expenses covered or are specific services excluded? Look for a policy that covers out-patient care. The trend is that more and more medical

and surgical procedures are being performed in out-patient settings.

9. Look for coverage that begins with the first day of hospitalization, including room and board, doctor visits and any medical/surgical procedures.

10. If you must cut corners, look for a no-frills major medical policy that pays most doctor and hospital bills but excludes routine physicals or prescription drugs.

11. How does the policy handle preexisting conditions? Some policies will cover after a waiting period.

12. To what extent are emergency room visits covered?

13. Look for policies that can be extended to a spouse or a dependent without a large increase in premium.

14. Pay your premium annually or semi-annually if you can. It costs less than monthly payments.

15. Check to see if you are covered away from home in case you need medical treatment while you are traveling.

16. Check exclusions. Common ones are prescription drugs, treatment for alcoholism, mental health services, ambulances and private-duty nursing.

17. Check restrictions to benefits. These are sometimes referred to as cost-containment clauses.

18. Remember there is a 10-day "free look" period after you receive the policy during which you can get a refund if you decide it's not right for you.

19. Make sure the policy is offered by a company that is committed to health insurance as a specialty, has an A or A+ rating by A.M. Best & Co., and at least $100 million in assets.

There are three basic types of health insurance: Hospital, major medical (catastrophic) and medical-surgical. The People's Medical Society book, *Getting the Most for Your Medical Dollar*, recommends that any policy you consider should cover the following items:

Major medical services should include:

Blood and components
(transfusions)
Cosmetic surgery (result of
accident/injury)
Dental treatment (result of
accident/injury)
Diagnostic tests (x-rays,
laboratory)
Durable medical equipment
(hospital bed, wheelchair
rental)
Home health care
Outpatient treatment services
(chemotherapy, radiation
therapy)
Obstetric services
Prescription drugs
Private-duty nursing

Prosthetic appliances
(limbs, eyes, orthopedic braces)
Psychiatric care services
Radiation therapy
Rehabilitation services
Respiratory therapy
Room and board (semi-private)
Skilled nursing facility care
Special care beds: intensive care
Surgery: surgeon/assistant
surgeon fees, supplies
Second surgical opinion
Surgery and supplies
Transportation (ambulance)
Therapist services: occupational,
physical, respiratory, speech
Transportation (ambulance)

Medical surgical insurance should include:

Allergy testing
Anesthesia: anesthesiologist/
anesthetist fees, supplies
Chemotherapy (including cost
of drugs)
Chiropractic care
Consultation services
Diagnostic services (in non-
hospital settings)
Doctor visits: office, hospital,
emergency room, home
Electrocardiogram (EKG)
Electroencephalogram (EEG)
Emergency accident care
Immunizations
Newborn care (routine)
Obstetric services (pre- and
post-natal care)
Oral surgeon's fee

Pathologist's fee (laboratory)
Physical examinations
Podiatry care
Psychiatric care services
Radiation therapy (radiologist's
fees, supplies)
Oxygen/oxygen supplies
Physician/surgeon services
Physical therapy
Prescription drugs
Surgery: surgeon/assistant
surgeon fees, supplies
Second surgical opinion
Surgery and supplies
Therapist services:
occupational, physical,
respiratory, speech
Transportation (ambulance)

The Agency on Health Care Policy and Research has a booklet with questions to ask about health insurance coverage and worksheet to help you compare plans. 800-358-9295.

Evaluating medical services

I recommend reading some of the publications of the People's Medical Society. It is a nonprofit consumer health organization dedicated to the principles of better, more responsive and less-expensive medical care. Membership costs $15 a year and includes a subscription to the newsletter. Contact them at 462 Walnut Street, Allentown, PA 18102, 215-770-1670.

Another organization is the National Women's Health Network. It is a nonprofit public-interest organization seeking to give women a voice in the U.S. health-care system. It functions as an information clearinghouse along with sponsoring action-oriented programs. National Women's Health Network, 1325 G Street NW, Washington, D.C. 20005, 202-347-1140.

Disability insurance

To supplement a state-operated plan, consider purchasing long-term disability insurance to cover 50 to 65 percent of your salary if you have a lengthy illness or become disabled. Carefully note:

1. Total amount the policy pays.
2. Length of the waiting period before payment.
3. How long the benefits continue.
4. Policy definition of disability. Some policies will pay if you are unable to work in your trade or occupation. Others will pay only if you are unable to work in any occupation.

Pension options

If you earn money in your own business as well as through employment as a temp working through several agencies, you may have both an IRA and a KEOGH plan. To enjoy the maximum benefit, both plans should be opened before December 31 of the tax year. Contributions to the plans will not be due until April 15 of the next year.

For the finer points, read up on the subject, talk to your tax professional as well as investment adviser to discern the best combination of options for you.

Independent Retirement Accounts (IRAs). Yearly, $2,000 of the temp income that is paid to you by agencies can be contributed to an IRA.

KEOGH plan. Plans with specified annual contributions (a money-purchase plan) limit the contribution to 13.03 percent of self-employed income. By combining it with a profit-sharing plan, you can set aside up to 20 percent of your qualifying income tax-free. Check into a defined benefit plan, as it might pertain to your situation, for even larger yearly contributions.

While the benefits situation is not ideal, it's also not necessarily as bleak as it is sometimes painted. The more competitive temporary employment companies will continue to come up with better benefits, whether or not the expected federal legislation comes to pass. People combining temporary employment with self-employment will have the pension options of both. In the meantime, while we're waiting for the best of all possible worlds to arrive, we investigate the less traditional sources and are innovative.

Further reading

The Complete Guide to Health Insurance: How to Beat the High Cost of Being Sick, Walker and Company, 1988.

Getting the Most for Your Medical Dollar, Charles B. Inlander and Karla Morales, Peoples Medical Society, 1991.

The Health Insurance Alternative (HMOs), Thomas R. Mayer, Perigee Books, Putnam, 1984.

Helpful publications

Consumer Reports publishes articles on insurance from time to time. Write or call, 101 Truman Avenue, Yonkers, NY 10703-1057, 914-378-2000.

Health Insurance Association of America (HIAA) has a free pamphlet listing all the state commissioner addresses and telephone numbers. Request one by calling 202-223-7808, or writing to P.O. Box 41455, Washington, DC 20018.

The Agency on Health Care Policy and Research has a booklet with questions to ask about health insurance coverage and a worksheet to help you compare plans. 800-358-9295.

Questions about continuation health insurance (COBRA):
Pension and Welfare Benefits Administration
Division of Technical Assistance and Inquiries
200 Constitution Avenue NW, Room N5625
Washington, DC 20210

Organizations with group medical insurance for members

Co-op America
1850 "M" Street NW, Suite 700
Washington, DC 20036
202-872-5307
Insurance questions: 800-331-2713 or 800-966-8467.

National Writers Union (NWU)
873 Broadway, Suite 203
New York, NY 10003-1209
212-254-0279

National Association of Temporary Services (NATS)
119 South St. Asaph Street
Alexandria, VA 22314
703-549-6287
Insurance questions: Temp Med 800-323-2106.

American Association of University Women (AAUW)
1111 16th Street NW
Washington, DC 20036
202-785-7700

Consumer organizations

Public Citizen Health Research Group (HRG)
2000 P Street NW
Washington, DC 20036
202-833-3000

National Insurance Consumer's Organization (NICO)
121 Payne Street
Alexandria, VA 22314
703-549-8050

According to *The Frugal Shopper*, NICO provides members with manuals and recommendations of specific companies (depending on type of insurance) that are doing a good job in giving insurance value and quality.

Conclusion

Good News/Bad News Revisited

· ·

The good news: There will be more jobs and more hiring in 1994. "The bad news:" The jobs will probably be for temporary positions. Industry spokespeople predict that the increased use of electronic databases and networks will decrease their need for recruitment staff. The electronic processing of information will, in turn, decrease the need for "core" middle management and support staff. To reduce costs, the federal government will continue to increase its use of contract, temporary and part-time workers. "Temp-to-Perm" will become more and more entrenched as a hiring practice.

The situation as I see it: Technology and temporary employment are here to stay. To thrive in this climate, it is necessary to learn how to use them both in a way that benefits you.

I fervently hope the information I have passed along about options and rights makes a difference in changing how you view temporary employment, and how you experience it. By exploring options and exercising rights, you will effect change where it is needed most, in the perception and exploitation of temporary workers by the ethically challenged.

May you have many interesting, productive, profitable temp adventures.

Resource List

Directories

Directory of Temporary Firms, Kennedy Publications, 800-531-0007.

National Trade and Professional Associations in the United States, Columbia Books, 202-898-0662.

Encyclopedia of Associations (2 volumes), Gale Research, Inc., 800-877-GALE.

Free publications

How to Read a Financial Report, Merrill Lynch brochure line, 800-637-7455.

Guide to Financial Instruments, Coopers & Lybrand, 212-536-2000.

How to Read The Wall Street Journal, The Wall Street Journal, Education Services Bureau, 609-520-4254.

Take Charge of Your Money, AARP, P.O. Box 2240, Long Beach, CA 90801.

How to File and Find It, free booklet from Quill Corporation, Business Library, 100 Shelter Road, Lincolnshire, IL 60069.

U.S. Government consumer publications: Write for a listing from Consumer Information Center, Pueblo, CO 81009.

Consumer publications: A resource for low-cost publications on any number of consumer-interest topics is your local Department of Consumer Affairs. Examples of pertinent titles in New York City are "Ranking Banking: The Consumer Score Card," and "Credit Card Interest Rates." Request a publications list by calling 212-487-4278.

The Agency on Health Care Policy and Research has a booklet with questions to ask about health insurance coverage and worksheet to help you compare plans. 800-358-9295.

Helpful books

Negotiation

Getting What You Want, Karen Anderson, New York, 1993.

Haggler's Handbook, Leonard Koren & Peter Goodman, W.W. Norton 1991.

Bargaining Games, John Keith Marnigham, New York, 1992.

Getting Past No, William Ury, New York, 1993.

Getting to Yes, Roger Fisher, New York, 1991.

Telecommunications

The Phone Book, a Consumer Reports Book by Carl Oppendahl. How to choose, fix and install equipment and everything you should know about getting the best service at the lowest cost.

Complete Guide to Lower Phone Costs, Consumers Checkbook, Washington, DC, 1984.

Home offices/Organizing/Self-employment

Conquering the Paper Pile-Up, Stephanie Culp, Writer's Digest Books, 1990.

Organizing Your Home Office for Success, Lisa Kanarek, Penguin Group, 1993.

Organized to Be the Best, Susan Silver, Adams-Hall Publishing, 1991.

Office at Home, Robert Scott, Scribner, 1985.

The Complete Work-At-Home Companion, Herman Holtz, Prima Publishing, 1990.

Making It On Your Own: Surviving and Thriving on the Ups and Downs of Being Your Own Boss, Sarah and Paul Edwards, St. Martin's Press, 1991.

The Home Office and Small Business Answer Book, Janet Attard, Henry Holt, 1993.

Self-employment

Breakaway Careers, The Self-Employment Resource for Freelancers, Consultants and Corporate Refugees, Bill Radin, Career Press, 1994.

Start Up, An Entrepreneur's Guide to Launching and Managing a New Business, 3rd ed., William J. Stolze, Career Press, 1994.

How to Avoid 101 Small Business Mistakes, Myths & Misconceptions, Gary L. Schine. Career Press, 1991.

Job search/Career

The Smart Woman's Guide to Resumes and Job Hunting, 2nd edition, Julie Adair King and Betsy Sheldon, Career Press, 1993.

The Smart Woman's Guide to Interviewing and Salary Negotiation, Julie Adair King, Career Press, 1993.

Thriving in Tough Times, Paul G. Fox, Career Press, 1992.

Adventure Careers, Alex Hiam and Susan Angle, Career Press, 1992.

Take This Job and Leave It, Bill Radin, Career Press, 1993.

Part-Time Careers, Joyce Hadley, Career Press, 1993.

101 Great Answers to the Toughest Interview Questions, Ron Fry, Career Press, 1994.

Cover Letters, Cover Letters, Cover Letters, Richard Fein, Career Press, 1994.

Finding a Job After 50, Terry Harty and Karen K. Harty, Career Press, 1994.

Successful Recareering, Joyce A. Schwarz, Career Press, 1993.

Business Letters for Busy People, Jim Dugger, Career Press, 1993.

Money matters

The Check Is Not In The Mail, Leonard Sklar, Baroque Publishing, 1990.

Penny Pinching, Lee and Barbara Simmons, Bantam, 1993.

The Frugal Shopper, Ralph Nader and Wesley J. Smith, Center for Study of Responsive Law, 1992.

If Time Is Money, No Wonder I'm Not Rich, Busy Investor's Guide to Successful Money Management, Mary L. Sprouse, Simon & Schuster, 1993.

Your Rights As a Consumer, 2nd ed., Legal Tips for Savvy Purchasing of Goods, Services and Credit, Marc R. Lieberman, Career Press, 1994.

Solving Your Financial Problems, 2nd ed., Richard L. Strohm, Career Press, 1994.

Life After Debt, Bob Hammond, Career Press, 1993.

The Consumer Reports Money Book, Janet Bamford, et al, Consumer Reports Books, 1992.

Making the Most of Your Money, Jane Bryant Quinn, New York, 1991.

Sylvia Porter's Your Finances in the 1990s, Sylvia Porter, Prentice Hall, 1990.

Lawyers/Legal

You Don't Always Need a Lawyer, Craig Kubey, et al., Consumer Reports Books, 1991.

Using a Lawyer...and What to Do if Things Go Wrong, Kay Ostberg in association with HALT, Random House, 1990.

Kill All the Lawyers, Sloan Bashinsky, Esq., Prentice Hall, 1986.

NOLO Press is the largest publisher of self-help law books. Call 800-992-NOLO for a catalog of listings. California residents, call 800-445-NOLO.

Medical insurance

The Complete Guide to Health Insurance: How to Beat the High Cost of Being Sick, Walker and Company, 1988.

Getting the Most for Your Medical Dollar, Charles B. Inlander and Karla Morales, Peoples Medical Society, 1991.

All things computer

Software templates: Simple Simon Says Series/TDA Help!, 721 132nd Street SW, Suite 202, Everett, WA 98204, 800-624-2101.

Utility software

IBM Environment
XTree Gold: XTree Company, 4330 Santa Fe Road, San Luis

Obispo, CA 93401, 800-388-3949 or 805-541-0604.

Magellan: Lotus Development Corp., 55 Cambridge Pkwy, Cambridge, MA 02142, 800-343-5414 or 617-577-8500.

PC Tools Deluxe: Central Point Software, 15220 NW Greenbrier Pkwy., Beaverton, OR 97006-9937, 800-888-8199 or 503-690-8090.

Q-DOS II: Gazelle Systems, 42 North University Ave., Ste. 10, Provo, UT 84501, 800-233-0383 or 801-377-1288.

MAC Environment

DiskTools Plus: Electronic Arts, 1820 Campus Drive, San Mateo, CA 94404, 415-571-7171, ext. 263.

DiskTop: CE Software, P.O. Box 65663, W. Des Moines, IA 50265, 515-224-1995.

Magazines

PC Magazine, P.O. Box 54093, Boulder, CO 80322, 303-447-9330.

PC Computing, Ziff-Davis Publishing Co., P.O. Box 50253, Boulder, CO 80321-0253, 800-365-2770.

Discounted software catalogs

Egghead Discount Software
800-EGGHEAD

800-Software, Inc.
800-888-4880

MacConnection
800-334-4444

PC Connection
800-243-8088

Ergonomic computer aids catalogs

AliMed Inc.
297 High Street
Dedham, MA 02026-9135
800-225-2610

Quill Corporation
717-272-6100

Discounted computer supplies catalogs

Lyben Computer Systems
313-649-2500

PC Connection
800-243-8088

MEI/Micro Center
800-634-3478

MacConnection
800-334-4444

800-Software, Inc.
800-888-4880

Dartek (Macintosh)
708-832-2100

Books

The Secret Guide to Computers 18th ed., Russ Walters (Pub.), 1993, 22 Ashland St., Somerville, MA 02144, 617-666-2666.

Peter Norton's PC Problem Solver, Peter Norton, Brady Books, 1993.

The "Dummy" series from I.D.G.:
  DOS for Dummies, Dan Gookin, 1993.
  Windows for Dummies, Andy Rathbone, 1993.

Macs for Dummies, David Pogue, 1993.

Voodoo Mac, Kay Yarborough Nelson, Ventana Press, 1993.

This Is the Mac. It's Supposed to be Fun, A. Naiman, J. Kadyk, Peachpit Press, 1993.

Organized to Be the Best, Susan Silver, Adams-Hall, 1991. Has terrific sections about business software and for organizing hard disks for both IBM and Macintosh.

Catalogs

Planning items
Caddylak Systems
510 Fillmore Avenue
Tonawanda, NY 14150
800-523-8060

Telephone products
Hello Direct
800-444-3556

Discounted office furniture
National Business Furniture, Inc.
222 East Michigan St.
Milwaukee, WI 53202
414-276-8511

Office Furniture Center
322 Moody St., Dept. 6001
Waltham, MA 02154
617-893-7300

Factory Direct Furniture
225 East Michigan St., Suite 11
Milwaukee, WI 53202-4900
414-289-9770

Frank Eastern Co.
599 Broadway
New York, NY 10012-3258
212-219-0007

Discounted office supplies
Quill Corporation
P.O. Box 1450
Lebanon, PA 17042-1450
717-272-6100
Customer Service (all regions): 708-634-8000

Staples, Inc.
P.O. Box 9328
Framingham, MA 01701-9328
508-370-8500

Reliable Office Supply
800-735-4000

Viking Office Products
800-421-1222

Schiller & Schmidt, Inc.
800-621-1503

Phar-Mor Corp.
800-522-5444

Organized living
Hold Everything
800-421-2264

Services/information

Agency Registration Resource (New York)

Baseline Recruiters Network, Inc.
800-BASELINE

Questions about continuation health insurance (COBRA)

Pension and Welfare Benefits Administration, Division of Technical Assistance and Inquiries, 200 Constitution Ave. NW, Room N5625, Washington, DC 20210.

Ordering stamps

800-STAMP24

You can call 24 hours a day, 7 days a week. You must pay with a credit card, MasterCard, Visa, or Discover. There is a $3 handling charge and it takes three to five days for delivery.

Cheap checks
Current
800-533-3973

The Check Gallery
800-354-3540

Custom Direct
800-272-5432

Artistic Checks
800-224-7621

Checks in the Mail, Inc.
800-733-4443

Long distance discount plans
AT&T
800-222-0300

Allnet
800-631-4000

MCI
800-444-3333

US Sprint
800-877-4646

Working Assets Long Distance
800-788-8588

Self-employment: Low-cost counseling

American Woman's Economic Development Corporation (AWED), 71 Vanderbilt Avenue, New York, NY 10169, 212-692-9009 or 800-321-6962.

SCORE or other SBA sponsored groups will give you their services, videos and publications, 800-827-5722.

The Entrepreneurial Center, *The Entrepreneur'sUltimate Resource Book,* Inc., 100 Manhattanville Road, Purchase, NY 10577, 914-694-4947, 1993.

Credit

TRW
National Consumer Relations Center, P.O. Box 2350, Chatsworth, CA 91313-2350.

Medical Information Bureau (MIB)
P.O. Box 105, Essex Station, Boston, MA 02112, 617-426-3660.

Credit Counseling
National Foundation for Consumer Credit, Inc., 8701 Georgia Avenue, Suite 507, Silver Spring, MD 20910, 800-388-CCCS.
    Contact to locate the nearest CCCS office.

Low-interest-rate Visa/MasterCards
Chevy Chase Federal Savings Bank
800-777-9901

AFBA Industrial Bank
800-776-2265

Consumer National Bankcard
800-862-1616

Publications

Consumer Reports, 101 Truman Avenue, Yonkers, NY 10703-1057, 914-378-2000.

Barrons and *Money* magazine both list credit cards with the current lowest annual percentage rates in each issue.

Consumer groups

Telecommunications Research and Action Center (TRAC)
P.O. Box 12038, Washington, DC 20005, 202-462-2520.

HALT: An Organization for Legal Reform
1319 F Street NW, Suite 300, Washington, DC 20004, 202-347-9600.

Bankcard Holders of America
460 Spring Park Place, Suite 1000, Herndon, VA 22070, 703-481-1110.

People's Medical Society
462 Walnut Street, Allentown, PA 18102, 215-770-1670.

National Women's Health Network
1325 G Street NW, Washington, DC 20005, 202-347-1140.

Public Citizen Health Research Group (HRG)
2000 P Street NW, Washington, DC 20036, 202-833-3000.

National Insurance Consumer's Organization (NICO)
121 Payne Street, Alexandria, VA 22314, 703-549-8050.

Public Citizen/Center for the Study of Responsive Law
P.O. Box 19367, Washington, DC 20036, 202-833-3000.

Organizations with group medical insurance available to members

Co-op America
1850 "M" Street NW, Suite 700
Washington, DC 20036
202-872-5307
Insurance questions: 800-331-2713 or 800-966-8467.

National Writers Union (NWU)
873 Broadway, Suite 203
New York, NY 10003-1209
212-254-0279

National Association of Temporary Services (NATS)
119 South St. Asaph Street
Alexandria, VA 22314
703-549-6287
Insurance questions: Temp Med, 800-323-2106.

American Association of University Women (AAUW)
1111 16th Street NW
Washington, DC 20036
202-785-7700

The unique makeup of each group taking one of my temp seminars determines the direction and content of the session. Of course, at the beginning I am able to ask questions and find out about their backgrounds and interests. At the end of a seminar, when my mind goes dry, I usually say to the class, "That's all I can think of to tell you. Let's have some questions. Ask me anything." And we're off and running again.

Here I am at the end of the book, but I don't know very much about you, the reader. I am hoping that the information I have passed along is useful to you. I am very interested in your feedback: your experiences, your tips, and certainly your questions. Please write me in care of Career Press, P.O. Box 34, 180 Fifth Avenue, Hawthorne, NJ 07507.

About the Author

Diane L. Thrailkill is president of DTA Automation Consulting, a firm providing business-related technical training and consulting services to corporations and small businesses. Ms. Thrailkill began working as an office temporary while writing her first book, and has been actively involved in the industry for the past seven years as "temp" as well as instructor.

Although Ms. Thrailkill is a native of San Diego, she was reared, nonetheless, as a "Southern Lady" by her transplanted parents. She had the unconventional childhood of a Navy brat, attending schools in several states, before growing up, more or less, in Southern California. She began her eclectic professional career as a counselor to teenage girls in a detention home. Later, she became an elementary school teacher, specializing in special education. After a move to New York, she worked for Young Presidents' Organization (YPO), designing seminars and programs that featured prestigious speakers and dignitaries. She left YPO to enter the corporate world at Citibank as an assistant vice president and technical trainer.

She graduated from San Diego University with a BA in sociology and minors in psychology and political science. She has written two other books.

Index

A.M. Best & Co., 166
Agency on Health Care Policy and
  Research, 168
Alternative Health Insurance
  Services (AHIS), 17, 164
American Institute of Certified
  Public Accountants, 154
American Woman's Economic
  Development Corp. (AWED), 117
Archives, computer documents, 85
Assets,
  liquid, 130
  nonliquid, 130
Association directories, 29
Attire, for registering with agency,
  29-30
Attorneys,
  fees and expenses, 157-159

finding, 155-157
when to consult, 155
Audits, red flags, 153

Back Stage, 28
Bankcard Holders of America, 133-134
Banks, 130-131
  financial rating, 131
Baseline Recruiters Network, Inc., 38
Beepers, furnished by agencies 25
Benefits, 160-171
  questions about, 37
Better Business Bureau, The, 133
Business expenses, categories, 151-153
Business records,
  how long to keep, 150-151
  self-employed, 151

Carpal tunnel syndrome, 92
Classified ads, finding temp
 agencies, 28
Co-Op America, health insurance,
 17, 164
Collection policy, home business,
 139-142
Company interviews, 46
Completed work, form, 74
Computer equipment,
 avoiding injuries, 92
 document holder, 92
 special-design keyboards, 92-92
 track ball mouse, 92
 wrist rest, 92
Computer passwords, breaking,
 89-90
Computer skills, increasing, 80-81
Computer software, discount
 catalogs, 93
Computer tips, 83-85
 advanced, 86-89
Computer viruses, 85
Computer-related assignments, 82-94
Computer-related injuries, 90-93
 catalog, 93
 preventing, 91-92
 symptoms, 91
Computers,
 compression software, 104
 home office, 103-104
Consolidated Omnibus Budget
 Reconciliation Act (COBRA), 17,
 162-163
Consulting services, hourly rates,
 128-129
Consulting, feasibility exercise,
 114-116
Consumer Credit Counseling
 Service (CCCS), 138
Continuation insurance, 162-163
Contracts, 155
Conversion software, 83

Corporation, 110, 115
Costs, start-up, 23
CPA Communications Council, 154
Creativity Checklist, 77
Credit,
 obtaining while temping, 132
 revolving, 132
Credit bureaus, 135-137
 disputes with, 137
 names of, 135
 obtaining credit report, 135-136
Credit cards, 132-135
 annual fee, 132, 134
 disputes, 134
 errors in billing, 134
 evaluating, 132
 grace periods, 133
 interest rate, 132, 133
 late fees, 133
Credit fraud, 138-139
Credit policy, home office, 140
Credit problems, 138
Credit rating, 135
Credit repair companies, 136
Credit report,
 correcting, 136
 disputes, 136-137
 obtaining, 135-136
Creditor, freelancer/temp as, 139-142

DBA certificate, 111, 113, 147
 jury duty, 113
Directory of Temporary Firms, 29
Disability insurance, 168
Diskettes, carrying blank, 84
Diversity, 10, 20

Efficiency, on the job, 71-81
Employee leasing, 161-162
Encyclopedia of Associations, 29
Equal Credit Opportunity Act
 (ECOA), 137
Executive Recruiter News, 29

Expenses, self-employment, 118-119

Fair Labor Standards Act:
  Minimum Wage and Overtime, 21
Federal Credit Reporting Act
  (FCRA), 137
Federal Deposit Insurance
  Corporation (FDIC), 131
Federal Fair Credit Billing Act, 134
Federal Fair Debt Collection
  Practices Act, 138
Federal Trade Commission, 135
Finder's fees, agency, 37
Forms of business, 110, 115
Freelance temping, 112-119
  finding clients, 113
  hourly rate, 112
  jury duty, 113
  setting rates, 114
  setting rates, 127-128
  taxes, 112
Frugal Shopper, The, 164
Full-time employment, before
  quitting, 109-111
Furniture, home office, 100

*Getting the Most for Your Medical
  Dollar,* 166
Giving availability,
  schedule conflicts, 62
  to agencies, 61
  when to call, 61

HALT, An Organization for Legal
  Reform, 159
Health benefits,
  lack of, 17
  temporary agencies, 162
Health Insurance Association of
  America (HIAA), 164
Health insurance, 163-168
  Co-Op America, 17
  evaluation, 165-166

finding, 163-164
HMOs, 163-164
major medical, 167
medical surgical, 167
National Writers Union, 17
ratings, 166
through membership
  organizations, 164-165
types of, 166-167
Health Maintenance Organizations
  (HMOs), 17, 163-164
  advantages, 164
  disadvantages, 164
Holiday pay rates, 126
Home Office Center, telephone
  consulting, 102
Home office, 95-107
  computers, 103-104
  credit policy, 140
  furniture, 100
  inventory of equipment, 97
  invoicing, 140-141
  mail, 104-105
  office supplies, 100-101
  organization, 97-100
  organizers, planners, 99
  psychological factors, 105
  tax issues, 147-148
  telephone consultants, 102
  telephones, 101-103
  zoning laws, 96
Homeowner's insurance, 96-97
Hourly rate, 45, 58
  attorneys, 157
  consulting services, 128-129
  freelance temping, 112
  freelance, 127-128
  holiday pay, 126
  job categories, 24
  questions about, 35
  questions about, 36
  temporary agencies, 125
  too low, 66

Identification, when registering, 30
If Time is Money, No Wonder I'm Not Rich, 130
Illness,
   job assignment, 69
   long-term assignment, 67-68
Independent contractors,
   qualifying rules, 149-150
   tax issues, 147, 148-150
Injuries, computer-related, 90-93
Internal Revenue Service, audits, 153
Invoicing, home office, 140-141
IRA, pension options, 168, 169

Job assignment, 44-59
   accepting, 62-63
   arriving early, 48, 80
   asking to be replaced, 64
   client wants private deal, 64
   declining, 46
   first impressions, 48-49
   illness, 67-68
   keeping track of information, 46-48
   on-the-job injury, 69
   on-the-job problems, 64-68
   preparing at home, 72
   problems, 57-58
   questions to ask, 45, 50-52
   simultaneous offers, 65
   upgraded, 69
   when to notify agency, 68-69
Job banks, 29
Job categories, hourly rates, 24
Job offer, from temp client, 68
Job security, 16
Job upgrade, 52

KEOGH, pension options, 168, 169
Kill All the Lawyers, 156
Kiplinger's Personal Finance, 110

Late shift, pay rate, 126

Legal issues, 144-159
Letters of agreement, 155
Liabilities, 130
Loans, obtaining while temping, 132
Long-term assignments, 55-57
Lunch breaks, 79

MacGuide, 83
Macro, computer functions, 84
MacUser, 83
Magellan, utility software, 83
Mail merges, computer functions, 85
Mail,
   buying stamps, 104
   home office, 104-105
   Postal Business Centers, 104
Major medical insurance, 167
Making It On Your Own, 116
Medical surgical insurance, 167
Money, magazine, 110
Money, 22-23, 125-142
Multiple agency relationships, 34, 60-70
   accepting better offer, 65
   giving availability, 61
   simultaneous offers, 65

Naming protocol, computer functions, 86
National and Professional Associations in the United States, 29
National Association of Temporary Services (NATS), 17, 22, 38
   health insurance, 163
National Foundation for Consumer Credit, Inc., 138
National Women's Health Network, 168
National Writers Union, 164-165
   computer-related injuries, 90-91
   health insurance, 17
   job banks, 29
Net worth, how to determine, 129-130

New York Law Review, 28
New York Times, The, 28

Occupational Outlook Quarterly, 120
Office supplies, home office, 100-101
Organizers/planners, 25-26, 61
  home office, 99
Overtime pay, 21
  computing rate, 126-127
  questions about, 37

Partnership, 110, 115
Paycheck, 18, 21, 67
  cashing, 127
  checking for errors, 127
  receiving by mail, 127
  questions about, 36
PC Computing, 83
PC Magazine, 83
Penny Pinching, 133
Pensions, 168-169
  temporary agencies, 162
People's Medical Society, 166, 168
Permanent placement fees,
  agencies, 37
Personal data fact sheet, 30
  sample, 32
Personality conflicts, 58
Postal Business Centers, 104

Quarterly taxes, 147

Referral bonuses, at temp agencies, 37
Registering with temp agency, 29-39
  identification, 30
  interviewing, 34-38
  multiple agencies, 34
  references, 30
  resume, 30
  testing, 31-34
Repetitive strain injuries (RSI), 90
Resume, 30
  temping as job-search, 121-122

Revolving credit, 132

S corporation, 110, 115
Schedule conflicts, with
  assignments, 62
Self-employment,
  counseling, 117
  expenses, 118-119
Skill-based, work force, 7, 13, 15,
  33, 125
Skills,
  dictation, 34
  graphic design, 34
  increase in, 69
  legal knowledge, 34
  proofreading, 34
  typing, 33
Small Claims Court, 142f
*Smart Woman's Guide to Resumes
  and Job Hunting, The,* 122
Socializing with permanent
  employees, 58
Software,
  help-line numbers, 85
  utility, 83
Sole proprietorship, 110, 115
Specialty temp agencies, 29
Stacker software, 104
Stamps, buying in bulk, 104

1099 form, 148
Tax ID, 147
Tax issues, 146-155
  audits, 153
  home office deductions, 148
  home office, 147-148
  independent contractors, 147-150
  part-time temping, 147
  paying quarterly, 147
  temporary agencies, 146-147
Tax professional, finding, 154
Tax Reform Act of 1986, 161f
Taxes, freelance temping, 112

Taxpayer Compliance Measurement, 153
Telecommuting, 95
Telephone answering machines, 23, 25
Telephone consultants, 102
Telephone list, company, 73
Telephone systems, company, 50, company, 54
Telephone, remote dialers, 54
Telephones, home office, 101-103
Temp Template®, 73
    sample, 53-54
Temping,
    advantages of, 20-21
    benefits to employee, 8-9, 10-11, 160-171
    disadvantages of, 14, 16-18
    diversity, 10, 20
    emergency measure, 9
    exploring career opportunities, 9
    flexibility, 21
    freelance, 112-119
    insider information, 10
    job-search, 119-122
    job security, 16
    lack of health benefits, 17
    legal issues, 144-159
    menial tasks, 18
    minimal stress, 20
    money matters, 125-142
    reentering work force, 10
    seasonal lows, 56
    subsidizing business, 9
    supplemental, 108-124
    wave of future, 8
    while receiving unemployment, 145
Templates, computer, 84
Temporary agencies, 27-39
    communications with, 39
    employee turnover, 63, 66

finding, 28-29
    health and pension benefits, 162
    how they work, 27
    plan benefits, 27
    relationship with temps, 27-28
    specialty, 29, 120
    taxes, 144
    unemployment insurance, 144-145
    worker's compensation, 146
Temps, misperceptions of, 16-17
Testing,
    at temp agency, 31-34
    software packages, 31
Thriving in Tough Times, 77
Timesheets, 18, 54, 67
    example, 19
    questions about, 36, 51
Training, from agency, 37
Transportation, questions about, 35-36

Unemployment benefits, 144-145
    temping while receiving, 145

Vacation pay, 37
Veribanc, bank-rating, 131

W-2 form, 146, 147
Wages, 22
Wake-up calls, 39
Wardrobe, 20, 29-30, 59
Word for Word, conversion software, 83
Worker's compensation, 145-146
Working Assets Long Distance, 102

Yellow pages, seeking temp agencies, 28

Zoning laws, 96